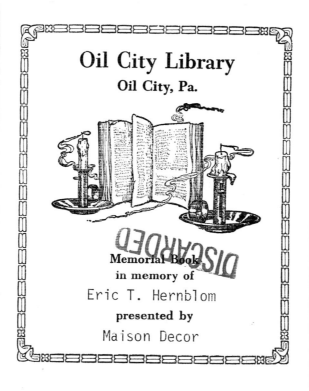

Oil City Library
Oil City, Pa.

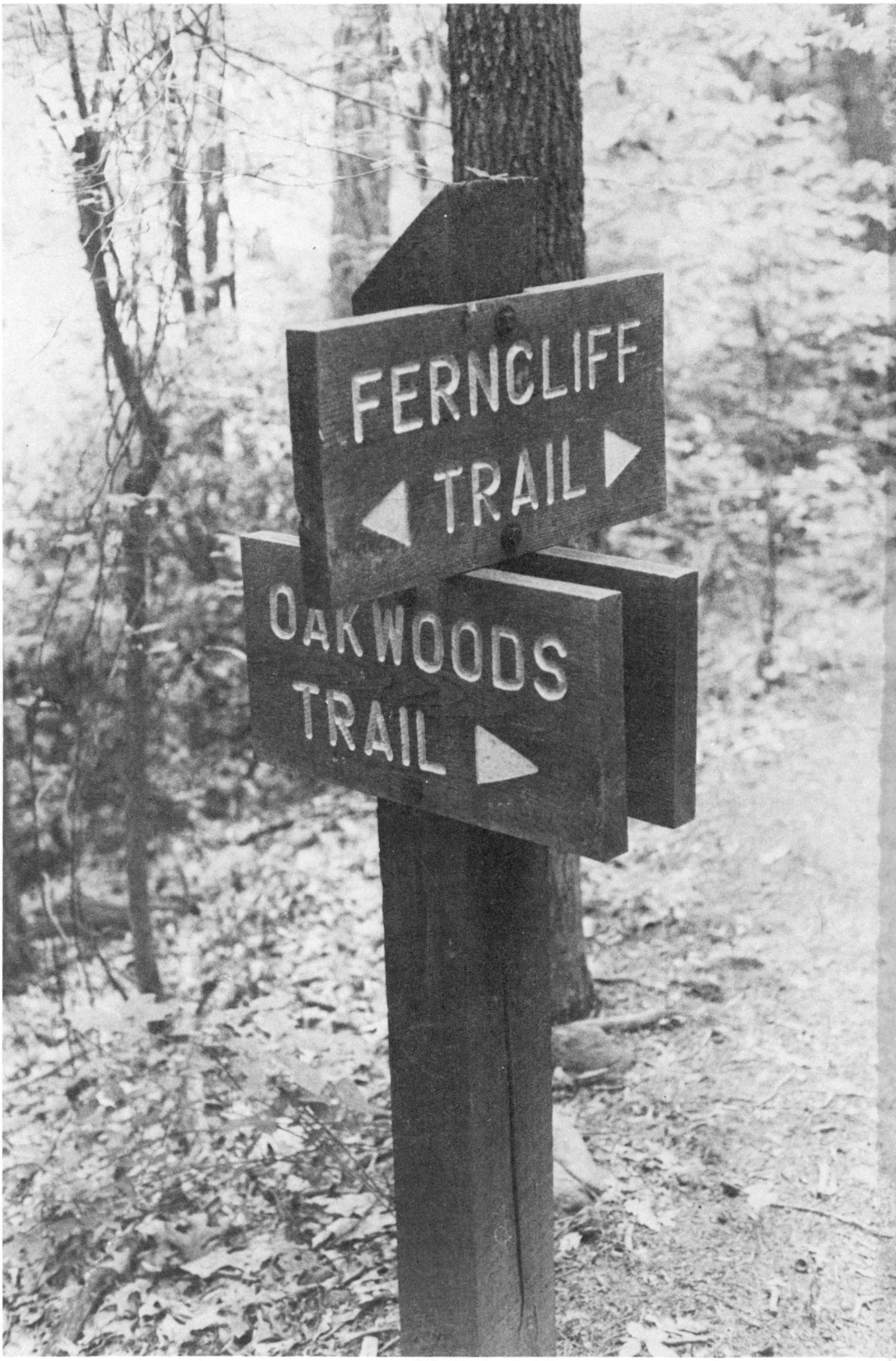
FERNCLIFF
TRAIL
OAKWOODS
TRAIL

Fifty Hikes in Western Pennsylvania

Walks and Day Hikes
From the Laurel Highlands
to Lake Erie

Tom Thwaites

Photographs by the Author

Backcountry
Publications
Woodstock, Vt.

An Invitation to the Reader

Housing developments, logging, mining, fires—these and other works of man and nature take their toll on hiking trails. If you find that conditions along any of these 50 hikes have changed, please let the author and publisher know so that they may correct future editions. Address correspondence to:

Editor, *Fifty Hikes*
Backcountry Publications, Inc.
P.O. Box 175
Woodstock, Vermont 05091

Acknowledgements

This book could not have been written without the help of many hikers living in western Pennsylvania. Among those who suggested hikes, served as hiking companions and provided trailhead services, car shuttles, shelter, food and information were Mary Ann and Steve McGuire, Glenn Oster, Bill Dzombak, Ray Gerard, Ruth and Norm Samuelson, Dave Gregg, Mark Place, Paul Wiegman, Jerry Bosiljevac, Bob Peppel, Mitch Dickerson and Roger Cuffey. I am particularly grateful to my wife, Barbara, who typed the manuscript. I also thank my editor, John Pierson, for his help and patience.

Library of Congress Cataloging in Publication Data

Thwaites, Tom.
  Fifty hikes in western Pennsylvania.

  Bibliography: p. 18
  1. Hiking—Pennsylvania—Guide books.
2. Pennsylvania—Description and travel—
1981-   —Guide-books. I. Title. II. Series
GV199.42.P4T49 1983   917.48   82-25277
ISBN 0-942440-10-2 (pbk.)

Published by Backcountry Publications, Inc.
Woodstock, Vermont

Printed in the United States of America

Design by Wladislaw Finne
Trail maps drawn by Richard Widhu
Cover photo by Marc Johnson

To all those volunteers
who build and maintain
foot trails in Penn's Woods.

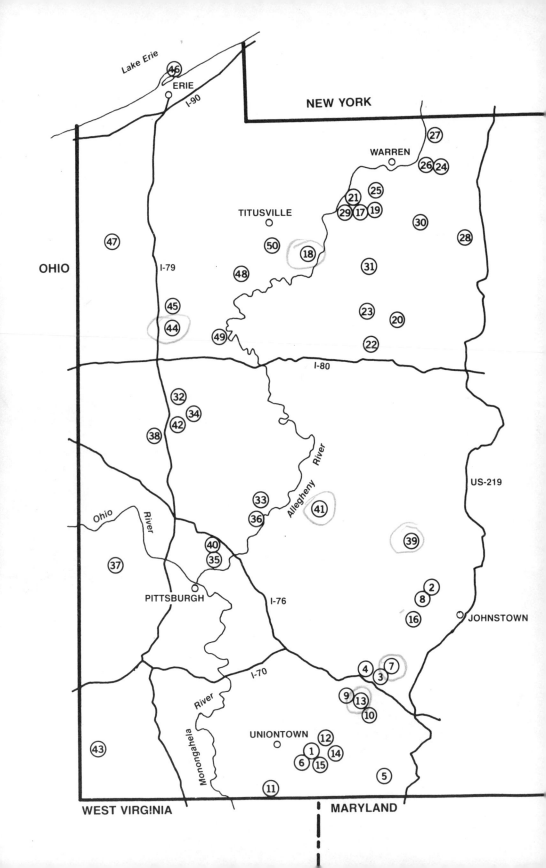

Contents

Erie and the North

Introduction

Hiking trails in western Pennsylvania are less rugged than those in the central and eastern parts of the state. This happy condition is a consequence of geology.

Today, western Pennsylvania is a plateau cut through by many river valleys. It was not always so. When the rocks in this part of the state were laid down in the Paleozoic Era, hundreds of millions of years ago, Pennsylvania was south of the equator and frequently under water. To the east there were high mountains, which probably resembled the Cordillera Blanco of Peru. Material eroded from these mountains was carried west to the shallow sea that covered much of North America. Hudson's Bay may be a relic of this ancient sea.

When this sea was fairly deep, limestones were deposited. When it was shallow, mud collected and shales were formed. When the sea retreated altogether, sandstones were laid down. Crossbedding of these sandstones indicates that they were deposited by streams which flowed across vast deltas that stretched from the mountains to what remained of the sea.

Later in the Paleozoic, swampy forests of tree ferns grew on these deltas and eventually became the coal seams of western Pennsylvania. Coal is only one of many energy resources in Penn's Woods. In 1859, the world's first oil well was drilled near Titusville. More than a century later, as you will see on several hikes, oil and gas wells are still being drilled.

After this great layer cake of rock had been formed, our continent collided with North Africa, forming the super continent Pangaea. Mountains were produced that probably resembled the Himalayas. The roots of these folded mountains, much eroded, form the ridge-and-valley region of central and eastern Pennsylvania. The folds reached into western Pennsylvania but were much gentler. By the time North America split off from Pangaea, these mountains had been eroded to a flat plain.

For reasons that are still obscure, the Appalachians were again uplifted, forming the plateau we see today. The anticlines of Negro Mountain, Laurel Hill and Chestnut Ridge were re-excavated by erosion and their tops form the highest elevations in Penn's Woods.

The rivers draining this plateau cut deep valleys into it. Most of them, including the Youghiogheny and the Allegheny, flowed northwest into the Saint Lawrence River where Lake Erie is today. The Ice Age changed this simple pattern. Glacier after glacier profoundly altered the northwestern part of the state, dotting the area with lakes, swamps and bogs and changing the course of rivers well beyond the reach of the ice. Some rivers were buried by glacial debris, and it is impossible to trace their preglacial routes. Other rivers had to reverse their flow. The Allegheny and Ohio rivers of today contain sections where water flows "uphill."

These great events formed the earth's crust into the setting for the hikes in this book. Rock layers on the western plateau are nearly horizontal, and even the anticlines have only a modest slope. In the ridge and valley region to the east, many rock layers stand almost on edge and have been shattered by erosion into enormous rock piles. For hikers the result is that slopes are gentler and trails less rocky in western Pennsylvania than in the central and eastern parts of the Commonwealth.

Hikers are generally restricted to public lands, and public lands are relatively scarce in western Pennsylvania. With roughly 500,000 acres, the Allegheny National Forest forms the largest tract of public land west of US 219. Next are some 250,000 acres of state game lands. Although organized trails are scarce, the game lands are widely distributed. One is even found just outside Pittsburgh. Hiking trails are also found in state forests, state and county parks and lands belonging to the Western Pennsylvania Conservancy. Many of the best hiking areas in western Pennsylvania—including large parts of Ohiopyle, McConnells Mill, Moraine and Laurel Ridge state parks, as well as Forbes State Forest and Jennings Nature Reserve—were purchased by the Western Pennsylvania Conservancy and transferred to public ownership. Sometimes it seems that a hiker would not be able legally to step off a road in western Pennsylvania were it not for the Conservancy.

As regards insects, Pennsylvania's location is a happy one. It is just far enough south to escape the black flies and just far enough north to avoid most of the ticks. But there are gnats that, while a distant second to black flies, nevertheless, try harder. Mosquitoes are abundant in the swampy areas. Deer flies can be a real nuisance as they try to carve off a steak.

Spring wild flowers are a particular delight of western Pennsylvania trails. Since the western part of the state is drier than the central part, this bounty must come from richer soils. The growing season is comprised of a few short weeks between the melting of the snows and the leafing of the trees. Wild flowers are not distributed uniformly along the trails; in some places there are hardly any, while in others they cover the ground like a late snowfall.

Hiking has much to recommend it as a recreational activity. It offers the cardiovascular advantages of jogging and bicycling, but with much less damage to the knees, ankles and feet than jogging and virtually no exposure to dangerous traffic. A jogger at age forty may have the best cardiovascular system of anyone using a wheelchair. Bicycling is still recreation. But as the supply of petroleum dwindles and synthetic fuels dance across the horizon at $5 a barrel more than oil, bicycling will become serious transportation. Hiking will continue to be recreational.

There are other benefits from hiking. Hiking brings us closer to nature and our roots in the natural world. Hiking reminds us that food does not come from the supermarket, wood does not come from the lumber yard and water does not come from the faucet. Hikers share the delights and dilemmas of those who cannot live without things that are natural, wild and free.

There are emotional benefits from hiking too. John Muir wrote: "Climb the mountains and get their good tidings. Nature's peace will flow into you as sunshine flows into trees. The winds will blow their own freshness into you, and the storms their energy, while cares will drop off like autumn leaves."

George W. Sears (1821-90) was Pennsylvania's pioneer conservationist and outdoor writer. "Nessmuk", as Sears

Ohiopyle Falls

was called, put it this way: "We do not go to the ... woods to rough it, we go to smooth it. We get it rough enough ... in towns and cities."

It's true! Whenever pressures and problems drive me to the woods, the miracle works again. A few hours of hiking, a view of the countryside, a long drink from a spring, and I can feel my problems drop away or shrink into perspective. I am freshly astonished.

About This Book

Detailed instructions are given here for 50 hikes on public lands or private lands where hiking is permitted. Since western Pennsylvania trails are, with few exceptions, poorly measured, all the hikes in this book were measured with a Rolatape model 660 M (2 meter circumference) measuring wheel. The distance given for each hike is how far you will walk to complete the hike as described. Where hikes can be shortened, instructions are included.

The hiking times were determined by my measured middle-aged pace. Those who have just taken up hiking may find their times exceed mine. Young hikers in good condition will have no trouble shortening them. But keep in mind that hiking is not a race and that it is the quality of the experience that counts.

The rise listed for each hike is the total amount of climbing obtained by adding together all the ups in an up-and-down hike. In some car-shuttle hikes—such as Maple Summit to Ohiopyle and Hemlock Run—the rise would be greatly increased if the hike were done in the opposite direction. In all cases the rise has been determined from the USGS 7½' topographic maps.

There are 21 short or introductory hikes in this book. They range up to five miles (8 km) long and up to three hours hiking time. Novice hikers should try

one or more of these short hikes before moving up to day hikes. Nineteen hikes range from five miles (8 km) to ten miles (16 km) and are classed as day hikes. Some of these could be turned into two-day backpacks, providing you can arrange to be dropped off and picked up and don't have to leave your car overnight at a trailhead. Cars left overnight may be drained of gas, ransacked or vandalized. In the Allegheny National Forest, check with the Allegheny Outdoor Club (see end of introduction for address) or the Chapman State Park Office (R.D., Box 1610, Clarendon, PA 16313, tel. 814/723-5030). They may be able to help you arrange trailhead service. Or consult Keystone Trail Association's Trailhead Transportation Guide, which lists public transportation to trails and state parks. Plans call for updating this guide every year, so make sure you have the most recent edition.

Finally, there are ten "boot-buster" hikes ranging from ten miles (16 km) to 13.6 miles (21.9 km). These are challenges for the most seasoned hikers. Again, some of them could be turned into backpacks.

Maps are listed at the end of each description. United States Geological Survey (USGS) maps are always listed but usually do not show the actual trails. State park maps are better for trails but do not show contours. What's more, state maps tend to be optimistic, sometimes showing trails that are no longer maintained or that may never have been cut. The best trail maps are those prepared by the organization responsible for trail maintenance. Copies of the Pennsylvania Recreation Guide and Highway map, which lists state parks and their facilities and activities, are available from the Office of Public Information of the Department of Environmental Resources. For information on where to order maps, see the list of addresses at the end of the introduction.

The fifty hikes are grouped in four geographic areas. Thirty-one hikes are concentrated in the Laurel Highlands and Allegheny National Forest areas. The remainder are in the Pittsburgh or Lake Erie areas, which are divided by I-80.

Equipment and Clothing

Hiking clothes should be comfortable. They do not have to be new or fashionable or expensive. In summer, when the primary task is keeping cool, hiking shorts and short-sleeved shirts are appropriate. The only equipment required is a day pack for carrying your lunch, canteen, insect repellent and rain gear, if the weather looks threatening. Don't try to cram these into your pockets.

Canteens are made of metal or plastic. With a little care, you can freeze the water in a plastic canteen in the freezer overnight and so provide yourself with a supply of ice water on the trail. The only advantage of a metal canteen is that you can put it directly on a stove in winter to thaw the ice trying to form inside. The only plastic canteen that ever failed me was bitten by a bear in the Smokies.

In fall and spring, the demands on clothing escalate. Temperatures may vary from near freezing in the morning to warm on a sunny afternoon. Also, the weather can turn hypothermic with little or no warning. These are the seasons when you will appreciate wool clothing. You may need one of the larger day packs to carry the layers you will shed as the day warms up, in addition to the items already mentioned.

Winter conditions are highly variable across western Pennsylvania. Snow depths may reach a meter or more in the Alleghenys and on Laurel Ridge, while other places may be bare. Deep snow requires snowshoes or cross-country skis; trying to hike without them leads quickly to exhaustion. Hypothermia is even more of a threat in winter. It can rain in winter, too. Yet there is as much beauty in the woods in this season as in the others.

Backpacking requires a lot more equipment than day hiking. You will need a sleeping bag, a backpack and some kind of shelter. Since you will spend about one third of your time in the sleeping bag, it's important to get one that's really comfortable. Mummy bags are much warmer than the traditional rectangular bags, but some people find mummy bags too confining. A bewildering variety of designs and materials is available, including some compromises between rectangular and mummy bags. For Appalachia's temperate rain forest, synthetic fillings such as Polarguard and Holofill are your best bets. They are slightly heavier than down but are cheaper and will keep you warm even if they get wet.

A good backpack is basically a collection of pockets of various sizes. The internal frame packs so popular today are designed for cross-country skiing and mountain climbing. For general purpose backpacking, the external frame pack is still the best. Backpacks should be fitted to your height. If a store wants to sell you a backpack without trying it on, take your business elsewhere. A padded hipbelt allows you to transfer 50 to 90 percent of the pack's weight directly to your hips, bypassing all those fragile discs in your back.

Adirondack type shelters are available only on the Laurel Highlands Trail. These shelters have an open front, a good roof and a fireplace. Elsewhere in western Pennsylvania, you will have

to carry your own shelter. A waterproof nylon tarp is the lightest and cheapest solution. However, when the bugs are really bad, you will need a tent with good ventilation. Again, a great variety of designs is available. The best advice is to rent before you buy.

An item of equipment that can greatly reduce your mark on the landscape is a backpacking stove. It leaves no pile of charcoal at your campsite and poses a minimal fire hazard. A variety of designs and fuels is available, and you should try several before investing in your own. When buying hiking and backpacking equipment, beware large retail chains. Seek out an outing store where the clerks know what they are selling.

Footwear

The most important and specialized part of a hiker's equipment is footwear. Shoes or boots for hiking must have good arch support and should also protect your feet from impact with rocks, roots, sticks and logs. Ideally, your footwear should also keep your feet dry in rain, snow or wet brush. Besides being cold and uncomfortable, wet feet develop blisters far faster than dry ones.

Leather hiking boots with lugged soles are almost ideal. Lugged soles look like a flexible waffle iron. These boots are available at outing stores, but they have been priced into hyperspace. Many hikers must search for cheaper alternatives and make a variety of compromises.

Walking shoes are low cut with leather uppers and some kind of rubber (even lugged) sole. Walking shoes must have good arch support. Usually they can pass for street shoes and are fre-

quently worn as such. They do not provide any ankle support and are suitable only for day hiking on good trails. Since they are low cut, it doesn't matter whether they are waterproof; the rain and snow have plenty of access anyway. Walking shoes are available at a wide range of prices, up to what real hiking boots cost just a few years ago. Old running shoes frequently see service as walking shoes, but their flexible soles let you feel every root and rock.

Another alternative is the ankle-high work boot. These were the traditional footgear of hikers before the European hiking boot arrived. Since they are generally made of split leather, they are difficult to waterproof. But work boots are available at a range of prices and with a variety of soles, including lugged. They are adequate for backpacking on good trails but do not provide as much ankle support as real hiking boots.

A third and more expensive alternative is the lightweight Goretex hiking boot. I've never worn them. Those who have used them claim they can really bounce along the trails. Others say Goretex boots aren't always waterproof.

Wait until you are sure the hiking bug has bitten before investing in a pair of real hiking boots. When and if you do, be sure to get boots of full grain leather with as few seams as possible. With good care, they should carry you along the trails for years to come.

The worst thing that can happen to leather shoes or boots is to get them soaked. Drying must be done slowly at room temperature. Even a few such wettings will greatly reduce the life of a leather boot. Purchase large enough boots so that you can wear two pairs of socks—a thin inner sock and a thick, mostly wool, outer sock—without cramping your feet.

Shadbush

Safety in the Woods

Compared with our roads and highways, the woods are very safe. Once you've parked your car and got a few strong trees between you and the nearest road, the chances of your being injured or killed have dropped by at least a factor of 10 and probably more like a factor of 100.

Still, there are dangers in the woods, and as they differ from those on the road and in town, they are worth spelling out. First are the hunting seasons for deer and bear. These usually take place in late November and early December, but they may vary from year to year. Check with the local office of the Game Commission (name may soon be changed to Wildlife Commission), a local newspaper or a hunter. The first day of deer season is the best day in the year *NOT* to be in the woods, or even out of doors, unless you are hunting deer. Even during deer and bear seasons, hunting is prohibited on Sundays. You could also hike in the "no hunting" portions of many state parks and in private wild life sanctuaries. But wear safety orange, just the same. Remember, hunters are outdoor people, too, and share many interests and concerns with hikers. Some of the great conservationists, such as Aldo Leopold, have enjoyed hunting.

A year-round threat to your safety in the woods is dirty drinking water. Most bacteria can be destroyed with chlorine or iodine, which are available in solid or liquid form. The liquids are much easier to mix with water in your canteen and greatly reduce the time you have to wait before you drink. The solid forms, however, have a much longer pack life. The best procedure is to fill your canteen with clean water before you leave home and then refill it only from tested supplies—out of a faucet or well at a picnic area or campground. But there are dangers in dehydration, so you must be prepared to treat untested water. An envelope of lemonade or some other drink mix, to cover the iodine or chlorine taste, deserves a place in your pack.

Poison ivy is abundant in western Pennsylvania and poses a threat to those who are unusually sensitive. In any case, you should learn to recognize poison ivy and reduce your contact with it. Yes, it does have three leaves. But so do a lot of other plants such as jack-in-the-pulpit, trillium, wild strawberry and blackberry. Of these, wild strawberry has the closest resemblance. The five-leaved Virginia creeper shares many of the same habitats as poison ivy but none of its bad characteristics. Those who are really sensitive to *Rhus radicans* may have to confine their hiking to trails where it is not found or seasons when it is dormant. An on-the-spot folk remedy for exposure to poison ivy is the sap of jewel weed *(Impatiens capensis),* which frequently grows near poison ivy. Drugstores sell a variety of poison ivy remedies including the traditional calamine lotion.

Stinging insects—hornets, wasps and yellow jackets—are another hazard in Penn's Woods. To people allergic to their stings, these insects can be life threatening. Yellow jackets nest underground, even in the middle of trails. You usually don't know you have stepped into a nest until you feel the first fiery sting. Then all you can do is run through some brush, swiping and swatting, to escape the vengeful horde.

Cold, wet weather presents yet another hazard. If you get soaked at any time when the temperature is below 10 degrees centigrade (50 degrees Fahrenheit), you are in trouble. Garments of wool, pile, Polarguard, Holofill, Thinsulate, etc. are your best defense against hypothermia. Even in the initial stages, before uncontrollable shivering sets in, your judgment and perception are dangerously and insidiously impaired. Be alert for signs of hypothermia in your companions. Slurred or incoherent speech, stumbling, falling and violent shivering are all signs of hypothermia. Treatment consists of warming the victim by getting him or her into a shelter and/or a sleeping bag. Alcoholic beverages will only make things worse.

Another threat from the weather is lightning. Don't stand under a tall tree or in an open field when lightning is around. For once, a car is about the safest place to be.

Three species of poisonous snakes are found in western Pennsylvania: timber rattlesnake, massasauga rattlesnake and copperhead. These snakes are no longer common. The rattlesnakes are threatened species and probably endangered, too. Every encounter between man and snake is almost invariably fatal—for the snake. Bites from poisonous snakes are serious but usually occur from handling. Innocent bites are extremely rare. Don't pick up or play with any snake, unless it is handed to you by the naturalist at the nature center. Snakes are members in full standing of western Pennsylvania wildlife and should be respected as such. Some are handsomely marked and are the easiest wildlife to photograph.

Lastly, beware of any wild animal that does not flee at your approach. Any animal that acts strangely must be suspected of having rabies. Should you be bitten by any wild animal, including a bat, make every effort to kill it so that its brain can be tested by the veterinary diagnostic laboratory in Harrisburg. Should the animal escape, you will have to undergo the entire series of shots for rabies.

All these hazards may make the woods seem dangerous, but they are rare. A little preparation and a pinch of common sense can make their probabilities comparable to that of being hit by a meteorite.

Respect for the Land and Its Inhabitants

Once you step off a road, your environmental impact increases dramatically. It used to be that man felt threatened by nature. But the numbers of our species have reversed this rule. Now it's the land and its wild inhabitants that are vulnerable. Carry out litter in pack or pockets, don't leave it to degrade the landscape. Some of our litter—bottles and aluminum cans—is of geologic permanence. Be careful with fire. Forest fires kill woods and wildlife. Never leave a campfire unattended; make sure it is dead before you move on. Try to build a campfire only where one has been built before. Don't smoke in the woods. Refrain from collecting wild plants or injuring live trees or shrubs.

Although hikers' use of the land constitutes the lightest of human impacts, even it can be overdone. Avoid overused hiking and camping areas. Those familiar with hiking in Allegheny National Forest will note the omission of Minister Creek Valley from this book. Minister Creek is the most heavily-used hiking area in western Pennsylvania and is omitted at the request of local hiking organizations. Many underused trails are included, so that the outfitters who have dispatched bus loads of backpackers to Minister Creek can now spread them around.

There are things you can do to improve hiking and backpacking in Penn's Woods. The Appalachian Trail was built largely by volunteers and is maintained exclusively by them. If the projected North Country trail from New York to North Dakota is ever to be completed, it will be built by volunteers. Join one or more of the organizations listed below, which are involved in building and maintaining hiking trails. A few people with hand tools can work miracles. Physically and emotionally, the rewards of trail work are as real as they are little known.

Hiking Organizations

Keystone Trails Association
P.O. Box 251
Cogan Station, PA 17728

Western Pennsylvania Conservancy
316 Fourth Ave.
Pittsburgh, PA 15222

Sierra Club, Allegheny Group
P.O. Box 7404
Pittsburgh, PA 15213

American Youth Hostels
Pittsburgh Council
6300 Fifth Ave.
Pittsburgh, PA 15232

Allegheny Outdoor Club
c/o Ruth Samuelson
205 Pickering
Sheffield, PA 16347

North Country Trail Association
P.O. Box 311
White Cloud, MI 49349

Other Books

Pennsylvania Hiking Trails, 9th Edition (1981) Keystone Trails Association.
Hiker's Guide to Laurel Highlands Trail, 3rd Edition (1981) Sierra Club, Allegheny Group.
Hiker's Guide to Allegheny National Forest, 2nd Edition (1982) Sierra Club, Allegheny Group.
Hiking Guide to Western Pennsylvania, 4th Edition (1978) American Youth Hostels, Pittsburgh Council.
Hiking Trails in the Mid-Atlantic States

(1976) by Edward B. Garvey, Contemporary Books, Chicago.
Trailhead Transportation Guide (1982) Keystone Trails Association.
Baker Trail Guide, American Youth Hostels. Pittsburgh Council.

Maps and Where To Get Them

United States Geological Survey Maps:
  From most outing stores or:
  U.S. Geological Survey
  1200 South Eads Street
  Arlington, VA 22202
  ($2.00 per map)
State park maps:
  From individual state park offices or:
  Office of Public Information
  Department of Environmental Resources
  P.O. Box 1467
  Harrisburg, PA 17120
  (tel. 717/787-2657)

Public use maps for state forests:
  From individual state forest offices or:
  Bureau of Forestry
  Department of Environmental Resources
  P.O. Box 1467
  Harrisburg, PA 17120

State game lands recreation maps:
  Pennsylvania Game Commission
  P.O. Box 1567
  Harrisburg, PA 17120
  (25¢ per map)

U.S. Forest Service maps:
  Allegheny National Forest
  Box 847
  Warren, PA 16356
  ($1.00 charge for Allegheny National Forest map)

Key to Map Symbols

————————————— main trail

• • • • • • side trail

P parking

Laurel Highlands

1

Ferncliff Natural Area

Distance: 2.1 miles (3.3 km)
Time: 1¾ hours
Rise: 200 feet (60 meters)
Highlight: Ohiopyle Falls
Maps: USGS 7½' Ohiopyle, Fort Necessity;
    state park map

Ferncliff is a peninsula surrounded on three sides by the Youghiogheny River, (pronounced: YAHK-ah-gainy). The river's name, like many others in Pennsylvania, is a white man's corruption of an Indian name. It is a magical area that reminds me of Point Lobos on the California coast. Perhaps it's the roar of the rapids and falls that reminds me of the surf. But it's also the sense of remoteness and isolation. Nearby Ohiopyle village and the rest of the state park seem completely cut off by the violence of the river. Around the Ferncliff Peninsula the Youghiogheny drops 90 feet in just one mile, producing Ohiopyle Falls and half a dozen rapids. Another point of resemblance to Point Lobos is the poison ivy that keeps you on the trails.

As with several other natural areas and reserves, Ferncliff Natural Area was originally acquired and operated by the Western Pennsylvania Conservancy. The painted trail signs that you may still find date from the Conservancy's tenure.

The peninsula has been formed by

Fossil Tree Fern

the gradual retreat of Ohiopyle Falls. At one time or another, the Youghiogheny may have flowed over the entire peninsula. Pot holes, such as you see at the brink of the falls, are also found above today's river level. The Youghiogheny River flows from the mountains to the south and brings with it seeds of southern plants. Thus Ferncliff is the northern outpost for many southern plants. Among these is the buffalo nut, a parasitic shrub that grows on the roots of mountain laurel. The Buffalo Nut Trail at Ferncliff is named after this shrub.

The trailhead can be reached only from PA 381. Turn west just north of the bridge over the Yough and before you reach the two tracks of the Baltimore and Ohio Railroad. Bear left at the sign into one of the parking lots. Follow the signs to the trailhead. The trail will take you under the old Western Maryland Railroad bridge to a trail junction and marker noting that Ferncliff was declared a National Natural Landmark in 1973. Follow the Ferncliff Trail as it bears left to emerge at the water's edge where a line is stretched across the river to keep boats, swimmers and fishermen from going over Ohiopyle

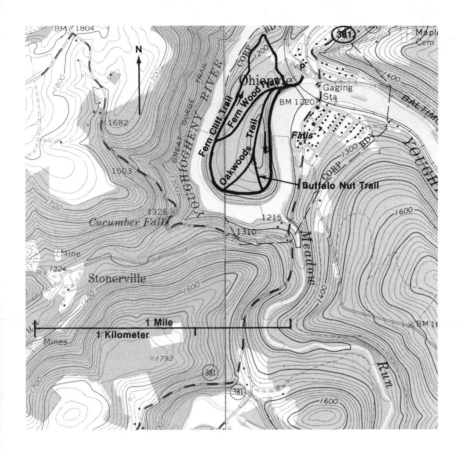

Falls. Near 0.2 mile (0.3 km) look for a fossil tree fern in the bedrock. It stretches almost entirely across the trail and is probably a lepidodendron or scale tree. Soon you see poison ivy edging the trail mostly on the right. Note driftwood logs lodged high above the normal level of the river. The shore here is bordered with thick jungles of rhododendron. When you reach the brink of the falls, the trail is forced out onto the ledges. Near 0.4 mile (0.6 km) turn left for the Fairbanks-Horix Overlook of Ohiopyle Falls. The falls are formed by the resistant Pottsville sandstone.

The overlook is from the brink of the cliff and has no guard rails, so watch your step. Perhaps it was from this very spot that George Washington viewed the falls in 1754 while trying to find a way to move men and supplies for the attack on Fort Duquesne. He may have thought that the reports of the waterfall had been exaggerated; waterfalls never lose much in the reporting process. But George was convinced and gave up the idea of water travel on the Yough. To the right, you can see the put-in place for today's travel on the lower Yough by kayak and raft.

Back on the trail you climb to the top of the cliff, tunneling through the rhododendron between large hemlocks and white pines. At 0.6 mile (0.9 km) you reach another overlook where the Buffalo-Nut Trail comes in from the right. A picturesque white pine stands at the edge of the cliff. A bit farther, look for an old lightning scar on a white pine to the left of the trail. You can hear but not see Entrance Rapids from this point.

Oakwoods Trail comes in from the right at 0.7 mile (1.1 km), and shortly, at a large white pine, there is a side trail that leads to the edge of the river. Back on the Ferncliff Trail, ignore the next side trail, as it does not lead to any good view. At 1.2 miles (1.9 km) keep left as the Fernwood Trail diverges to the right. The trail returns to the cliff side, and you can hear another rapids below. An unsigned trail goes right at 1.5 miles (2.4 km), and shortly you turn left to an overlook, which provides a good view of rapids.

At 1.7 miles (2.7 km) bear right, and the trail will take you through a stand of hemlocks set about with boulders. From here, you can hear the roar of yet another rapids—probably Railroad Rapids. Next, you turn right to take the trail back across the base of Ferncliff Peninsula. Along the way you cross a small meadow and then bear left at the trail junction to return to your car.

For an unusual hike, follow the Takeout Trail loop to the foot of Railroad Rapids. Many river runners portage and put in again just below the falls. From the takeout you can see the Western Maryland Railroad bridge across the Yough. Note how much higher this bridge is than the one just scarcely 600 yards away at the village of Ohiopyle. That's how much the river has fallen in its trip around the Ferncliff Natural Area.

Charles F. Lewis Natural Area

Distance: 3.9 miles (6.2 km)
Time: 2¾ hours
Rise: 1,000 feet (305 meters)
Highlights: Views, waterfalls
Maps: USGS 7½' Vintondale;
    Gallitzin State Forest Natural Area map

The Charles F. Lewis Natural Area is a small portion of Gallitzin State Forest located on Laurel Ridge northeast of the Conemaugh Gorge. Dr. Charles Fletcher Lewis, for whom the area is named, was a newspaperman, conservationist and first president of the Western Pennsylvania Conservancy.

The natural area, although only 384 acres, is suitably wild and rugged. It is reported to have an abundance of rattlesnakes and I think one buzzed at me on my hike. Reptiles and amphibians are protected within the Natural Area. I also encountered a pileated woodpecker... At one point in the trail, I was confronted by a large black object. Then it moved and snorted and I realized it was a bear. At the sound of her snorts, her cubs (two at least) shot up a basswood tree, and I fumbled in my pack for a telephoto lens. But Mama snorted again, the cubs quickly returned to the ground, and by the time I was ready, they had all vanished into the woods. The trails are steep, rocky, and wet, so hiking boots are in order.

The Charles Lewis Natural Area is located on PA 403 in the Conemaugh Gorge, 3.5 miles south of U.S. 22 and 5.9 miles from the PA 56 junction in Johnstown. There is plenty of parking space.

To start the hike, head across the open picnic area and pass through the arch at the start of the orange-blazed Clark Run Trail. At 130 yards bear right up the steps. You will return on the log bridge over Clark Run to your left. From 275 yards you can see the best of the waterfalls on the Run. Trees growing in this part of the valley are basswood, beech and yellow birch. The steepest part of the climb is over at 0.5 mile (0.8 km), and soon you cross a charcoal flat or hearth. There are many more of these old charcoal flats elsewhere on Laurel Ridge. They supplied charcoal to the iron industry in the nineteenth century. An old woods road is reached at 0.8 mile (1.3 km). The Clark Run Trail turns left on this grade. To the right the grade leads out along the face of Conemaugh Gorge for about one mile to a vista, but much the same view can be obtained from Rager Mountain Trail where it crosses a power line.

To pick up the Rager Mountain Trail, jog right on the old road and head up the flight of steps. The Rager Mountain Trail is also orange-blazed. It climbs the ridge between Clark Run and Con-

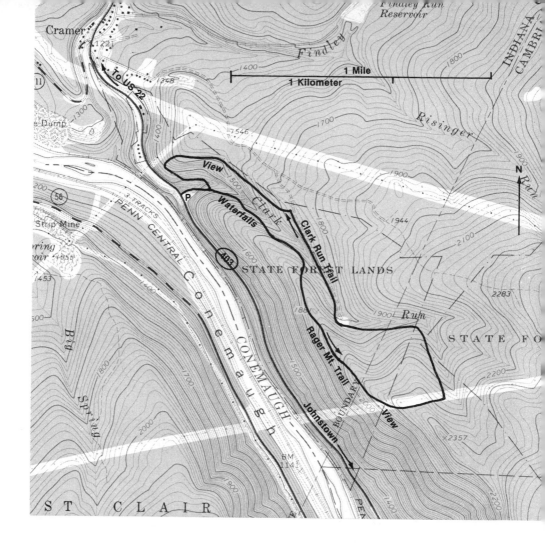

emaugh Gorge. The power line providing the view is reached at 1.5 miles (2.4 km). You can see the television and fire towers on Laurel Ridge above Johnstown as well as the great slash of the gorge itself.

The Rager Mountain Trail continues on the far side of the highline swath, but to stay within the Natural Area this hike turns left along the power line. An access road running along the left side of the power line makes a good trail. Towards the bottom of the first ravine turn left on an obvious but unmarked

old woods road. Trees along this part of the trail are tulip, cucumber, and black birch. At 2.3 miles (3.6 km) turn left on another old woods road. From here you may be able to hear Clark Run again. Next, the trail passes through a grove of Hercules club. This shrub has the largest leaves (doubly compound) of any woody plant in the state, and at least as many thorns. Next, keep left along the side of a meadow, and at its far side turn right on the Clark Run Trail. Cross the run on stepping stones or on the ruins of the footbridge and follow the

Conemaugh Gorge

old road along Clark Run. The Rager Mountain Trail comes in from the right at an obscure and unsigned junction along this section of trail. Many side streams cross this section of trail and some of them follow it.

A critical turn is reached at 2.9 miles (4.6 km). Ahead you can see a gate blocking the old road at the edge of the state land. So watch closely for the Clark Run Trail to turn left. This new trail is rough and rocky as it cuts across the side of Clark Run Valley. This is an ideal place to meet rattlesnakes, so watch your step. At 3.3 miles (5.2 km) you top out along the white-blazed state forest boundary. A view rock to the left of the trail looks out across Clark Run Valley into Conemaugh Gorge.

Back on the trail, you soon turn left and descend steeply at times through very rocky terrain. At 3.8 miles (6.0 km) turn left on a road, which is the old route of the paved highway. The original highway bridge over Clark Run is long gone, so you must bear left off the old highway and proceed upstream to the log bridge. Across the bridge you bear right on the trail you came in on and are soon back at your car.

This hike could be extended considerably by following the Rager Mountain Trail beyond the power line and across the top of Rager Mountain itself.

Wolf Rocks Trail

In-and-out distance: 4.3 miles (7.0 km)
Time: 2¼ hours
Rise: 160 feet (50 meters)
Highlight: Panoramiç view
Maps: USGS 7½' Ligonier, Bakersville; Forbes
   State Forest Public Use map; State Forest Ski
   Touring and Snowmobile Trail System map

Natural overlooks are rare in Pennsylvania. Since no part of the state approaches timberline in elevation, rocky cliffs provide the only overlooks. Such rocky cliffs are uncommon, and trees below frequently grow tall enough to shut off the view. Laurel Hill is broad and flat on top, further reducing the chances for a natural overlook. This hike visits an overlook on Laurel Hill that surmounts all these obstacles and provides a 180-degree panorama above Linn Run.

The hike starts from the Laurel Summit picnic area, which is also the access point for the Spruce Flats Bog. The origin of this depression on top of Laurel Ridge is obscure. The bog had progressed to a mature stand of hemlock, which is frequently confused with spruce, when it was logged in 1908. It turned out that the transpiration of the trees had been responsible for removing the water from this undrained depression. With the trees gone, the water table rose and the bog was reformed. All efforts at reforestation have failed; to become forest again, the bog must repeat the natural succession.

The Laurel Summit picnic area is 5.8 miles south of US 30 on the Laurel Summit road. Turn at the sign for Laurel Mountain Ski Resort. The picnic area can also be reached from PA 381 at Rector via the Linn Run Road. A water pump, picnic shelter and tables, as well as pit toilets, are available at the picnic area.

The roads in the picnic area appear to have been spurs on the Pittsburgh, Westmoreland and Somerset railroad, which was built across Laurel Ridge at the turn of the century to serve the Byers-Allen sawmill at Ligonier. Chartering the railroad separately from the sawmill established it as a "common carrier" and permitted it to condemn right of way when needed. Although the P, W & S eventually reached Somerset, using part of the right of way built for the South Penn railroad (Vanderbilt's Folly), its name can only have sprung from nineteenth-century optimism, for it never had the remotest hope of reaching Pittsburgh. The South Penn right of way was owned at that time by the Baltimore and Ohio, which did not grant the P, W & S permission. Building the P, W & S without permission was an act of corporate chutzpah. The grades across Laurel Hill were stiff, but rod locomotives were able to negotiate them. Geared shay locomotives were used only on logging spurs where grades hit twelve percent.

The Wolf Rocks Trail is fairly flat and has rocks only at the far end. Ordinary walking shoes should be fine for this hike. From the vicinity of the water pump, head back through the picnic area and bear left to the corner where the blue blazes begin. The trail is also marked with red blazes for cross country skiing. You will see that parts of the trail have been relocated to make it better for skiing. At 0.2 mile (0.3 km) you cross a pipe line swath. The trail continues along the fringes of the Spruce Flat Bog where rhododendron thrives. Soon you cross a tiny stream on a

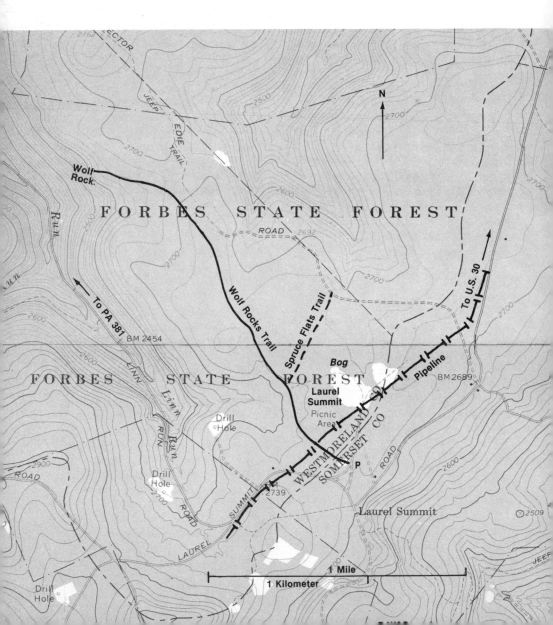

View from Wolf Rocks

bridge, and at 0.6 mile (1.0 km) the red-blazed Spruce Flats Trail goes right. The new sections of the Wolf Rocks Trail are blazed in a darker shade of blue, but the lighter blue blazes on the bypassed sections have not been obliterated. Near 1.3 miles (2.0 km) you can see the old Rector Edie road to the right.

At 2.0 miles (3.2 km) you cross a newly-bulldozed jeep road, and at 2.2 miles (3.5 km) you reach Wolf Rocks. You can see down Linn Run Valley and across to Chestnut Ridge in the west. You can also see up Fish Run Valley, just across from you, and up to the top of Laurel Hill itself. Rhododendron and

mountain ash trees grow around Wolf Rocks, adding to its appeal.

According to the map you could vary your return to the picnic area by cutting over to the Rector Edie road, either from where you see it or via the Spruce Flats Trail. In either case, you would end up following the pipe line to complete your return, and that route is almost as wet as Spruce Flats Bog itself. If you decide to follow the old railroad grade into the bog from the picnic area, wear sneakers.

Other nearby hikes are at Linn Run State Park (Hike 4) and along the Laurel Highlands Hiking Trail near Beam Rocks (Hike 7).

Linn Run State Park

Distance: 4.6 miles (7.4 km)
Time: 2¾ hours
Rise: 850 feet (260 m)
Highlights: Waterfalls; old cobblestone quarry
Maps: USGS 7½' Ligonier; state park map

Linn Run State Park is a small state park on the western side of Laurel Hill. To the south is Forbes State Forest. These lands had been clearcut by the time the state purchased them from Byers and Allen Lumber Company in 1909. The Pittsburgh, Westmoreland and Somerset Railroad, built for the logging, had started many fires on the cutover lands. The deer had all been killed. So there was criticism of the state for spending money on such wasteland. Today, we are the beneficiaries of the state's foresight. Deer were reintroduced from Michigan and New York. The forest reclaimed the briar patches and fern fields. The Linn Run Road has almost obliterated the Pittsburgh, Westmoreland and Somerset Railroad. In the 1930's the Civilian Conservation Corps built many of the structures in the park. More recently, these have been rebuilt by the Youth Conservation Corps.

The Youth Conservation Corps. has also built an attractive hiking trail up Grove Run, over the height of land to the east and down Boot Hollow Run. The trailhead is located at Grove Run Picnic Area, which is on the Linn Run Road three miles southeast of the small village of Rector (on PA 381). Ordinary walking shoes should be fine for this short hike.

Drive through the picnic area, which is equipped with a piped spring and restrooms, and park in the small area at the far end. The Grove Run Trail begins here. It is signed and blue-blazed. Pass around the vehicle gate and then step across the outlet from a spring to the right of the trail. The Grove Run Trail was built as a nature trail complete with numbered posts. Near the beginning most of the posts are missing. The trail starts out easily along an old logging road, but at 0.4 mile (0.6 km) you bear right and climb up the side of the valley. Trees along this section of the trail are tulip, red oak, and red maple. Farther along, the stream, which often flows underground in the lower parts of the valley, returns to the surface. After you cross Grove Run on a bridge just below a small pool, swing left and climb up the valley of a tributary. Next, you pass a waterfall that can be seen and heard in the narrow valley below you. Trees along this stretch are basswood, sugar

Pool on Grove Run

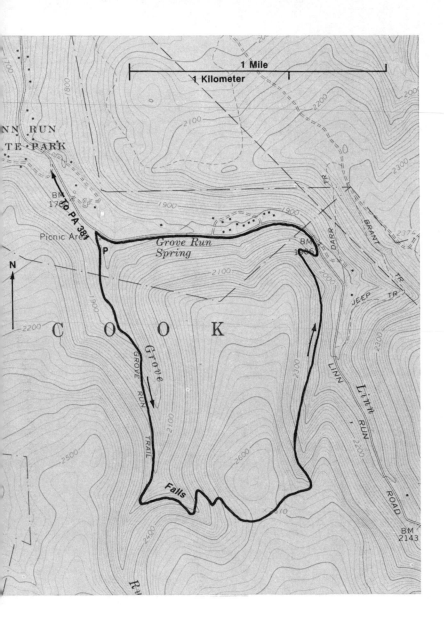

maple, beech and striped maple *(Acer pennsylvanicum),* the only tree named after Penn's Woods. Soon you cross the spot where most of the tributary comes down across mossy ledges to the right of the trail; then at 1.3 miles (2.0 km) you turn left across the remainder of the stream and continue climbing across the hillside. The trail switchbacks up the steep slope. The abundance of green briar, a vine-like thorny plant, discourages you from shortcutting the switchbacks. Despite its thorns, green briar or cat briar, is food for deer, bear, grouse, turkey and smaller animals. On these drier slopes, chestnut oak is the most common tree.

There is a trail register at the end of one switchback. If the register had been placed closer to the road, almost certainly it would have gone the way of most of the numbered trail posts. Take the time to register. You still have some climbing ahead, so this is a good place for a breather.

After another switchback, you reach the top of the hill at 1.8 miles (2.9 km) and cross the Quarry Trail, which is part of the Laurel Highlands snowmobile trail system. Soon you cross a watercourse and start down into Boot Hollow. The trail cuts along the side of the steep slope, where there should be some leaves-off views across Linn Run Valley. In summer the green curtain is opaque. At 2.9 miles (4.7 km) you cross the corner of an old blowdown. Wild grapevines have taken over and produced a tangle that is now encroaching on the surrounding trees. The wild grapes provide food and cover for wildlife, particularly birds. This spot is marked by post no. 19.

You cross the snowmobile trail again at 3.1 miles (5.0 km), and soon you come to post no. 20, which marks the site where a tornado touched down for 30 seconds in the spring of 1974. See how this opening has stimulated new growth. Next you cross a stream, then you switchback to the right, passing through a hemlock grove and recrossing the stream. There will be some cliffs coming up on your right, which are part of an old bluestone quarry. The quarry

supplied cobblestones for paving the streets of Pittsburgh. The owners of the Pittsburgh, Westmoreland and Somerset Railroad thought the quarry would permit their railroad to survive the logging era. But cobblestones lost out to asphalt and concrete.

Turn left on the Quarry Trail, pass the vehicle gate and turn left again on Linn Run Road. There is a large parking area on the far side of the road, so a car shuttle could be used. However, the road back through the park is fairly good. First you pass the park office. Stop in and tell them you've enjoyed hiking in the park. Hikers, who disappear into the woods, are invisible users of state parks. Park officials may not know you've even been there, if you don't tell them. Next, you pass some rental cabins, and at 4.3 miles (6.8 km) you come to Grove Run spring. This is the real thing. You've heard of other "undrinks". This is the "unwater"— unchlorinated, unfluoridated, unpolluted—pure Pennsylvania mountain spring water. All you can drink for free. At 4.4 miles (7.1 km) you cross Grove Run itself and turn left into the picnic area for the short walk back to your car.

Two short hikes are found farther up Linn Run. On the north side, the Darr Trail and Brant Trail make a short loop, using part of the old Rector Edie Road. On the south side, the Fish Run Trail leads to the remains of the Pittsburgh, Westmoreland and Somerset Railroad. You can also make a loop by returning along Fish Run. See also Hikes 3 and 7.

Mt. Davis Natural Area

Distance: 5.8 miles (9.4 km)
Time: 3¼ hours
Rise: 740 feet (225 meters)
Highlight: Highest point in Pennsylvania
Maps: USGS 7½' Markleton; public use map—
    Forbes State Forest

Of the states in the Appalachian Mountains, Pennsylvania has the lowest high point. At 3,213 feet, just under 1,000 meters, it is a grave disappointment to peak baggers. Yet Mt. Davis has character. Unlike the highest point of one midwestern state, it is not in the middle of a cornfield. The trees are stunted. Even on a sunny day it has an alpine feel. But the weather is frequently foul; even in midsummer there can be fog so thick that you can't see the ground from the top of the 50-foot observation tower.

Mt. Davis Natural Area is 581 acres of state forest land surrounding the high point on Negro Mountain. The peak is named for an early settler and former owner of the area, while legend has it that the mountain is named for a black man who was killed there when he and his companions were set upon by Indians or by a wounded bear or other wild animal. The incident may have taken place to the south, in Maryland, where Negro Mountain reaches a higher elevation.

This is a circuit hike using the Mt. Davis picnic area on LR (Legislative Route) 55008 as a trailhead. The picnic area is 9.2 miles from Meyersdale,

which in turn is about 22 miles south of Somerset on US 219. In Meyersdale, turn west on Broadway Street and follow the occasional signs to Mt. Davis or High Point. A bit west of town you can see Negro Mountain ahead of you, particularly the large microwave relay tower which is just across the road from the picnic area. Coming from the west on US 40, turn north on PA 523, travel 1.5 miles, then turn east in Listonburg. Pass High Point and Deer Valley lakes to reach the picnic area and trailhead at 10.7 miles from Listonburg. The high point of Mt. Davis itself could be used as an alternative trailhead, which would shorten the hike by 0.4 miles. Outhouses and a pump for drinking water are available at the picnic area. The picnic area and much of the land covered on the Tub Mill Run Trail were added to Forbes State Forest after the USGS map was printed.

To start your hike, head uphill to the top of the picnic area and then turn left on the High Point Trail, passing a spring to your right. At 0.2 mile (0.3 km) turn left on the blue-blazed Tub Mill Run Trail, and at 0.6 mile (0.9 km) jog left across the Shelter Rock Road to continue on the same trail. There are

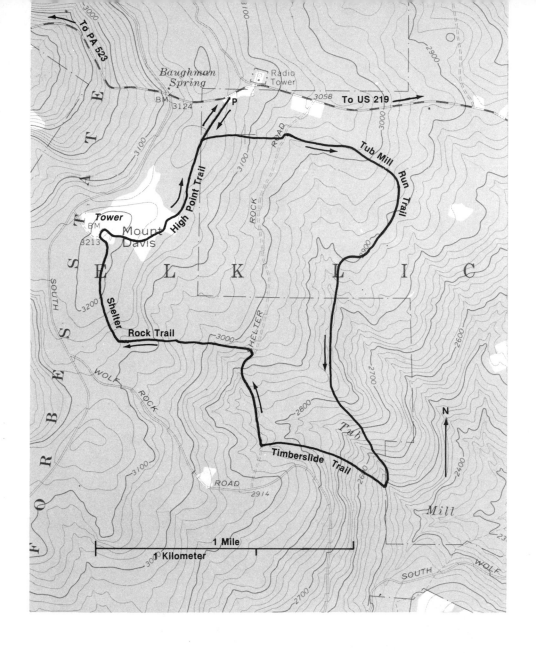

rhododendron as you continue to descend gently. At 1.7 miles (2.7 km) you reach the edge of a small cliff set about with mountain laurel. Soon you cross a nameless tributary of Tub Mill Run and continue through the forest to 2.6 miles (4.1 km) where the trail parallels Tub Mill Run itself, which jumps from rock to rock under the rhododendrons. When the water is even moderately high, this is a delightful stream. At 2.9 miles (4.6 km) you cross Tub Mill Run. Even with

A GEOLOGIC FEATURE

MT. DAVIS

MT. DAVIS 3213 FEET ABOVE SEA LEVEL
IS THE HIGHEST POINT IN PENNSYLVANIA.
THE EROSION-RESISTANT SANDSTONE AT THE
SURFACE BELONGS TO THE POTTSVILLE GROUP
FORMED ABOUT 230 MILLION YEARS AGO.
THESE LAYERS OF SEDIMENTARY ROCK WERE
PUSHED UP AS AN UPFOLD 200 MILLION YEARS
AGO DURING THE UPHEAVAL CALLED THE
APPALACHIAN REVOLUTION.

moderately low water the stepping stones are covered so the crossing can be exciting.

The trail continues briefly down the far side of the run before climbing to an unsigned junction with the Timberslide Trail. A flurry of blue blazes tempts you to descend further, but turn right and start the climb up to Mt. Davis. There are occasional blue blazes along the Timberslide Trail. At 3.3 miles (5.3 km) you pass a small clearing to the right and then cross an underground stream, which you can hear flowing beneath your feet. At 3.4 miles (5.5 km) you turn right on the Shelter Rock Road, which is closed to vehicles. Soon you pass Wildcat Spring, a few paces to the right of the road. The water comes up through the sand so fast that it looks as if it were boiling. Next, you cross a bridge over Tub Mill Run—not nearly so exciting as your last crossing—and at 3.8 miles (6.1 km) you turn left on the Shelter Rock Trail. This trail is very straight, and a good deal of work has been done on the footway. You cross Tub Mill Run for the last time, and at 4.1 miles (6.6 km) you reach the top of the hill. The trail takes you through a forest of stunted trees: black gum, pitch pine, oaks, aspen, sassafrass and maples. It's not just the poor soil on the Pottsville sandstone, but the many ice storms and the generally inclement weather that keeps these trees so small.

At 4.8 miles (7.7 km) the Mt. Davis Trail diverges to the right, providing a very short loop on top of Mt. Davis. Next you turn left and then right on the paved road to reach the base of the observation tower. If weather permits, climb the tower for the commanding views in all directions. The view from the tower includes stone circles to the north. These are formed when frost heaves elevate an area of soft soil, and over the years the rocks gradually slide down the sides. The ridge is so flat that points to the north and south appear higher than Mt. Davis. Careful surveying shows them to actually be lower. But it is a convincing optical illusion.

Continue to the exhibits and cross the paved road to pick up the High Point Trail. The Mt. Davis Trail comes in at 5.0 miles (8.0 km), and soon you are back under larger trees. At 5.6 miles (9.0 km) you pass the junction with the Tub Mill Run Trail, and it is but a short distance to the parking lot and your car.

Additional hiking opportunities are found south of the Natural Area on the Livergood, Wolf Rock, and Laurel Run trails, totalling over four miles.

Cucumber Falls

Distance: 5.9 miles (9.5 km)
Time: 3½ hours
Rise: 840 feet (260 m)
Highlights: Waterfall, spring wild flowers
Maps: USGS 7½' South Connellsville, Mill Run,
   Fort Necessity, Ohiopyle; state park map

A tram road is a railroad that uses geared locomotives. These were developed for the nineteenth-century logging industry. But coal mining also involved heavy loads and steep grades, problems frequently solved with a tram railroad. This hike uses the grade of one such old railroad, now part of the Great Gorge Trail along Cucumber Run and the Youghiogheny River.

This hike is best done with a short car shuttle so as to avoid walking on a narrow paved road. Drive west on LR (Legislative Route) 26071 for 1.4 miles from the log cabin on PA 381 in Ohiopyle State Park. Turn right at the top of the hill and leave one car at Tharp Knob picnic area. Then drive back downhill 1.0 mile to the Cucumber Falls parking area.

There is a bridgeless crossing of Cucumber Run near the start of this hike. This can be avoided by crossing the one-lane bridge above Cucumber Falls and turning right on the Great Gorge Trail at the far side. Numerous wet spots and rocks make hiking boots better for this hike. However, with a little care, good walking shoes should do.

To start, descend the steps on the north side of the road. At the first level you get the best view of the falls of the Cucumber. Continue down the switchbacks to the Yough and a junction with Meadow Run Trail. Turn left and hunt for a spot where Cucumber Run is funneled between two large rocks. Here you can jump across. Then keep left, pick up the yellow blazes, and follow the Meadow Run Trail as it climbs away from the Yough and ends at the Great Gorge Trail.

Turn right on this old tram road and follow it past one of the old mines. At 1.0 mile (1.6 km) you have to get off the railroad grade to cross a ravine. The bridge is long gone. The best displays of spring wild flowers are found along the Great Gorge Trail. Somewhere beyond here the railroad ended, but a road continued to more mines farther along the gorge. At 1.4 miles (2.2 km) you reach a junction with the Beech Trail, and the Great Gorge Trail climbs the hill to the campground. You could shorten this hike by following the Great Gorge Trail to the Kentuck Trail. Another trail connects with the Western Maryland Railroad grade. Because the

Cucumber Falls

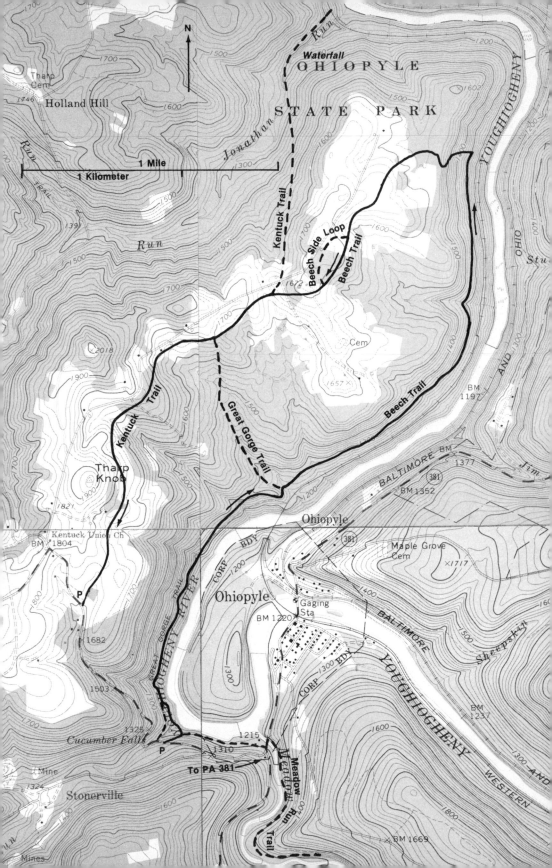

bridge is unsafe, and there is no view from the abutment, it is better to continue on the white-blazed Beech Trail. On the Beech Trail, at 1.6 miles (2.6 km), you come to another old coal mine and at 2.1 miles (3.4 km) to a rock overhang, a good place to wait out a shower.

The Beech Trail turns left, uphill, at 2.6 miles (4.2 km) and soon reaches the base of some larger cliffs with more overhangs and a small waterfall. The trail turns left along the base of the cliffs and then switchbacks to the top. It continues to climb, and towards the top of the hill it passes among some very large beech trees. After reaching the top of the hill, the trail continues through old woods. At 3.5 miles (5.6 km), it enters a meadow. Note the old apple trees growing in the meadow. Toward the top of the meadow there are good views to the east and north. A cross-country ski trail intersects the Beech Trail just inside the fringe of trees.

Continue ahead where the Beech Loop Trail goes off to the right. The Beech Trail has been frequently wiped out here by the graded ski trail. So you might as well follow the ski trail. Note the trees that are slowly converting these old fields into woods: dogwood, hawthorn and crab apple. At 3.8 miles (6.1 km) the Beech Side Loop rejoins the trail on the right, and shortly you pass between the vacant nature center on your left and the campground am-

phitheater on your right. You are at the edge of the campground, and there is no easier place to get lost. Pay close attention.

Bear right on the paved road past the RV dump station, where recreational vehicles empty their holding tanks. As you approach the campground contact station, keep left. An unsigned but mowed path climbs the hill and provides another view. At 4.1 miles (6.6 km) you bear left on the red-spot-blazed Kentuck Trail. The Kentuck Trail passes through meadows and patches of woods. The Great Gorge Trail junction is reached at 4.3 miles (6.8 km). At several places the trail borders old fields. Along one stretch the hill drops off very steeply to the left, and soon you reach Tharp Knob picnic area with drinking water, restrooms and the car you left here earlier.

This hike could be extended considerably if, instead of following the Beech Trail at 2.6 miles (4.2 km), you cut downhill to the Western Maryland railroad grade. Turning left, you could then walk the railroad grade past where Bear Run comes in from Fallingwater and around the Bear Run Peninsula to Jonathan Run. There is a waterfall a little way up Jonathan Run, and a trail leaves the run here, climbing to the campground and the Kentuck Trail. Another possibility is the remainder of the Meadow Run Trail which is known for its spring wild flowers.

7

Laurel Summit

Distance: 6.9 miles (11.2 km)
Time: 4 hours
Rise: 380 feet (115 m)
Highlights: View, Laurel Highlands Trail
Maps: USGS 7½' Ligonier; Hiker's Guide to
    Laurel Highlands Trail, maps 7 and 8; State
    Forest Ski Touring and Snowmobile Map

In the past few years, cross country skiing has been the fastest-growing winter sport. But in the Laurel Highlands, it has been restricted by a shortage of suitable ski trails. Snowmobiling started here years before and took over all the old roads and trails. Although snowmobiles are not permitted on the Laurel Highlands hiking trail, the trail could be skied only by experts. Now trails are slowly being cleared and blazed for cross-country skiers. The ski touring/snowmobile map for this area is available from Forbes State Forest, 132 West Main St., Ligonier, PA 15658. This hike uses several of the new ski trails, together with the Laurel Highlands Trail, to make a circuit on the broad crest of Laurel Hill. No single map shows all the trails used on this hike.

The trailhead is on the Laurel Summit Road 2.2 miles south of US 30. Turn off US 30 at the sign for the Laurel Mountain Ski Resort. Park in the cross-country skiing lot across from the side road to the resort. Although the footway is generally good and the hike is not all that long, the wet spots on some of the ski trails are very wet indeed. Hiking

boots are in order. When the skiers use these trails, the wet spots are frozen solid.

To start the hike, keep right at the east side of the parking lot and take the red-blazed Summit Trail to the right. All the different colored blazes along this hike are rectangles or try to be. Next you cross a power line swath and at 0.3 mile (0.4 km) turn right on a jeep road which actually follows a pipe line. Although it has a sign identifying it as the East End Trail, this is not the East End Trail shown on the maps. At 0.4 mile (0.6 km) there is a junction of the power line, pipe line and Laurel Summit Road. Turn left and find where the Summit Trail enters the woods. Once you've found it, you see that it is well cleared and easy to follow. Although you soon pass a sign for the Albert Trail junction, continue on the Summit Trail which takes you through thickets of rhododendrons.

At 1.0 mile (1.6 km) you bear right on the yellow-blazed Laurel Highlands Trail, then cross the headwaters of Spruce Run on a log bridge. Next, the red-blazed ski trail diverges right, but you

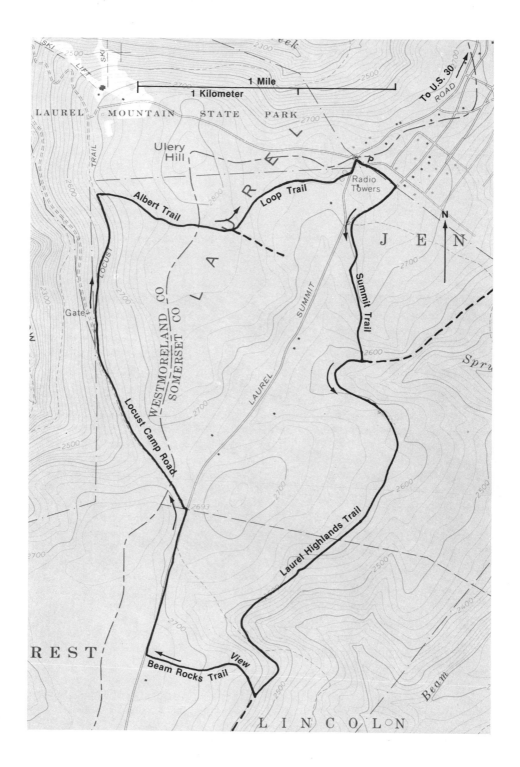

should keep left. Soon you cross another stream on a log bridge and then bear left at the crossing of the Spruce Run Trail. You pass milepost 42 at 1.9 miles (3.0 km), and later you cross another ski trail. Next you reach the blue-blazed Berma Trail (sometimes Burma, on the maps) which goes directly to the Laurel Summit Road.

At 2.8 miles (4.4 km) the blue-blazed Beam Run Trail goes right, and you cross Beam Run itself. As you pass milepost 41 at 2.9 miles (4.6 km), you can see large rocks off to the right.

Soon the trail passes among them. Note that the blue blazes from the Beam Run Trail have continued along this section of the Laurel Highlands Trail. Watch carefully for the Beam Rocks Trail to turn right, as the post sign may still be missing. This turn is at 3.1 miles (4.9 km). The blue blazes soon lead you out to Beam Rocks and a good view across the broad summit of Laurel Ridge. Only off to the extreme right can you see the ridge drop away.

Follow the blue-blazed trail out to the Laurel Summit Road and turn right

along the road at 3.7 miles (5.9 km). Along the road you pass the trailhead for the Beam Run Trail, and at 4.2 miles (6.7 km) you turn left on the Locust Camp Road, dodge around the gate, and soon come to a timber improvement cut on your right. Only the straight and healthy trees have been left, in the hope that they will now grow faster. Soon you pass the site of the portable sawmill, marked by a large pile of sawdust, after which you return to the unimproved forest. Posted private land will appear shortly on the left.

At 5.1 miles (8.1 km) bear right on the Locust Trail. This is obviously an old logging railroad bed, most likely a spur of the Pittsburgh, Westmoreland and Somerset. The railroad climbs steadily but with a very modest grade.

At 5.6 miles (9.0 km) turn right on the Albert Trail. It is marked with red blazes as well as faint blue blazes. You need to watch for both to follow this trail, especially where there is no ground cover. The well cleared path is easy to follow through the mountain laurel, and a faint trace can usually be seen through the ferns, except where there have been recent blowdowns. The only really difficult section is where there are neither ferns nor laurel. Soon you come upon yet another kind of marker. These are red metal rectangles nailed to trees. Each marker sticks out to the side of the tree and so can be seen in profile. At 6.2 miles (9.9 km) you turn left on the Loop Trail, which is also marked with red metal tags and red paint blazes. Parts of the Loop Trail are very muddy, particularly where it circles around a rock knob to the left. A radio antenna is then passed, and immediately beyond, you turn left on the Laurel Summit Road. The parking lot is just around the bend.

Additional hiking in this area is available on the Wolf Rocks Trail (Hike 3) and at Linn Run State Park (Hike 4).

Conemaugh Gorge

In and out distance: 7.2 miles (11.5 km)
Time: 4 hours
Rise: 1200 feet (365 meters)
Highlight: Views
Maps: USGS 7½' New Florence and Vintondale;
   Laurel Ridge State Park map; Hikers Guide to
   the Laurel Highlands Trail, map 12.

One of the most prominent geographic features in western Pennsylvania is Laurel Hill. Stretching north from the Mason-Dixon Line and reaching elevations up to 3,000 feet, Laurel Hill forms a barrier to transportation across the state. Even its modest elevation is enough to measurably alter the climate on the hill. The annual temperature averages about three degrees Celsius lower, and total precipitation about 50% higher, than flanking areas. Snowfall can be five times as great.

Nature provided only two gaps through Laurel Hill, the Youghiogheny in the south and the Conemaugh in the north. Presumably these gaps were eroded by water as the land was slowly uplifted. The streams may appear inadequate for this task, but a stream does almost all its eroding when it is at flood stage.

Conemaugh Gorge must have presented an appalling sight during the Johnstown Flood of 1889. On the afternoon of 31 May the South Fork Dam burst. The ruins just east of US 219 are preserved as a national historic site. The flood swept through Johnstown kill-ing over 2,200 people. Much of the debris piled up on the old stone bridge in Johnstown, but there must have been more that was carried through Conemaugh Gorge. Bodies were found as far downstream as Pittsburgh.

In the nineteenth century both the Pennsylvania Canal and the Pennsylvania Railroad used the Conemaugh Gorge to get through Laurel Ridge. Later railroad development appears to have obliterated the canal in the gorge. The highways go right over the top. Even the turnpike climbs over the ridge in preference to using the old South Penn railroad tunnel. As there is no practical car shuttle, this is an in-and-out hike. The views are best when the leaves are off.

The trailhead for this hike is reached from PA 56. The turnoff (on the south side of PA 56) is 1.0 mile east of the junction of PA 711 in Sewerd and about 4.8 miles from Johnstown. The parking area is 0.4 mile from PA 56 and drinking water is available from a fountain in

Conemaugh Gorge

summer. A sign warns that cars are left at the owners' risk. The footway is good to excellent so walking shoes should be adequate for this hike.

Moving into the woods on the yellow-blazed Laurel Highlands Trail, you quickly come to a concrete marker embedded in the ground and labeled number 70. This is the last milepost on the Laurel Highlands Trail. Actually the Laurel Highlands Trail isn't quite 70 miles long, so the last mile was shortened by about one-third to accommodate milepost 70.

Next, you encounter a trail register. Even day hikers should register, as funding for maintenance depends on usage. Overnight use of the shelter areas requires reservations, which can be made by calling (412) 455-3744. Shortly, the trail crosses a jeep road to

the Big Spring reservoir which can be seen to the right. A great many communities get their drinking water from the flanks of Laurel Ridge.

At 0.6 mile (1.0 km) there is a wooden-poled power line. To the left, you can catch a glimpse of Conemaugh Gorge. But the best views are to come. After crossing a jeep road in back of a spoil bank, you come to milepost 69. The jeep road crosses once again as the trail approaches the edge of the gorge. Note the rhododendrons growing on the moist north-facing slope of the gorge. Soon you reach the first real view. Across the gorge you see the Charles F. Lewis Natural Area and the valley of Clark Run. Towering above is Rager Mountain. Note the mountain laurel, for which the ridge is named. There is evidence of quarrying along

this section. At one point, a large steel bolt protrudes from a sandstone boulder. At another point, there are cinders in the trail, presumably from a steam engine at the top of a funicular used to lower stone to the bottom of the gorge. Small trees here are sassafrass, and large ones are tulip.

At 1.5 miles (2.3 km) you cross the corner of a jeep road leaving the quarry area and its views. Soon you come to a 500 kilovolt power line on steel pylons. To the left, there is a spectacular view of the gorge, while on the right, you can see the coal-fired power plant producing the power. You come next to milepost 68 and just beyond that, there is a large red oak growing on the brink of the gorge. At about 2.5 miles (4.0 km) the trail levels off but still follows the edge of the abyss. Milepost 67 is passed at 2.8 miles (4.4 km). Small trees growing along here are striped maple, and many of the large ones are black cherry, the premier northern hardwood. It has a dark, flaky bark. The ground underneath may be covered with the pits of the cherries of past years.

At about 3 miles (5 km) the trail starts to climb again with leaves-off views out the east end of the gorge, where you can see parts of Johnstown. Rager Mountain can also be seen beyond the gorge.

The trail soon swings away from the edge of the gorge and heads south near the crest of Laurel Hill. A jeep road is reached at 3.6 miles (5.8 km), which marks the end of the views. Lower Yoder firetower is 0.6 mile farther. It has been fenced off because of repeated vandalism, though, so its views of Johnstown and Laurel Ridge are no longer available. Turn and retrace your steps to your car. Hiking a trail in the other direction frequently doubles what you see.

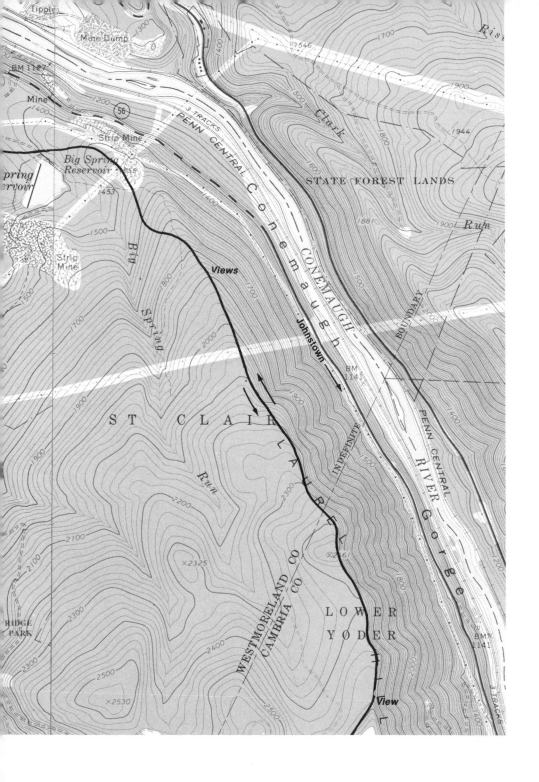

Roaring Run Natural Area

Distance: 7.2 miles (11.6 km)
Time: 4½ hours
Rise: 960 feet (300 meters)
Highlights: Mountain stream, spring wildflowers
Map: USGS 7½' Seven Springs; State Forest
   Natural Area map

At 3,000 acres, Roaring Run is the largest state forest natural area in western Pennsylvania. It is part of the mountain streams tract that was purchased by the Western Pennsylvania Conservancy on the western slopes of Laurel Ridge and transferred to Forbes State Forest in 1975. Before the Conservancy acquired the tract, a good deal of logging had been carried out. It will take a century for the second- and third-growth hardwood forest to mature, but hikers of the late twenty-first century have a real treat in store.

This hike is laid out so as to avoid private land and recent logging near Boy Scout Camp Alliquippa, which obliterated trails in that area. Further, the trailhead can be reached entirely on paved roads. Owing to frequent crossings of Roaring Run, this hike should be attempted only during low water, and hiking boots are strongly recommended. The best time to visit Roaring Run for spring wild flowers is the last two weeks in April.

To reach the trailhead from PA 31, turn south on PA 381 and PA 711 at Jones Mills. After 1.1 miles turn east (left) on County Line Road at the gas station in Champion. Then go 1.8 miles to a small parking area on the left side of the road.

To start your hike, walk around the vehicle gate and head up the old woods road. Most of this hike is on similar old roads, and although the natural area is closed to motor vehicles, the ruts you will see in every wet spot show frequent motorcycle incursions. The trail is marked with faded blue blazes.
At 0.3 miles (500 m) you continue ahead where the South Loop Trail comes in from the right. You will return on this trail at the end of your hike. Further on, the old road crosses a culvert over a small stream. Cat briars flourish in the undergrowth along this section. They can make off-trail hiking very painful but are a favorite food of the deer. Where the trail cuts across a steep slope, note the boulders that have slid down the mountain.

At one mile (1.6 km) you cross Roaring Run itself and turn right upstream. This is the first of 28 stream crossings, and if this one does not appear feasible, you had best retreat and just hike up and back the South Loop Trail.

After the second stream crossing,

look for rhododendrons growing along the run. They should bloom in early July. Near 1.4 miles (2.3 km) look for a basswood tree growing along the run. Basswood can be recognized by its nearly circular or heartshaped leaves and its seeds which are borne in a cluster attached to a narrow leaflike blade or sail. Although basswood is classed as a hardwood, its wood is actually soft and suitable for carving. Iroquois Indians carved masks from a living tree, and when the outside was finished, split the masks off to hollow out the back. Using live wood must have increased the medicine or spiritual power of the mask.

A small meadow is reached at 1.8 miles (2.8 km), and you soon cross two small streams from the south. After this, the crossings of Roaring Run become more frequent. At about 2.5 miles (4 km) the trail really starts to climb and the stream is much reduced in size. There is a double crossing at 3.0 miles (4.8 km). These crossings are some of the very few on this hike that could be avoided without excessive bushwhacking. The next ten crossings come in quick order as the valley here is constricted by steep banks. At the last of these crossings look for the stonework of an old road to the left of the trail. You are now approaching the very obscure junction with the South Loop Trail, so pay careful attention. The Roaring Run Trail climbs the steep bank and keeps to the left of the stream for 200 yards. Then it descends to the stream which may be dry at this point. At 3.5 miles (5.6 km) this is the junction with the South Loop Trail, which is behind you and to your right. There is a sign spiked to a tree, but you can't see it unless you turn around. Should you miss this obscure junction, landmarks beyond it are as follows. First, an obscure trail (the North Loop, but no sign) climbs up the hill to the left. Next, the Roaring Run Trail bears right, leaving what has now become a jeep road behind. Finally, at 3.7 miles (6.0 km) you would hit the Fire Tower Road at the edge of the Natural Area. At whatever point you realize you have missed the junction, turn back. The sign for the South Loop Trail is now facing you.

The first mile (1.7 km) of the South Loop Trail has rocks and blowdowns, but at least it isn't so vulnerable to motorized incursions. It is also comparatively well blazed and has a fairly good footway. The South Loop dips into a couple of small ravines, but for the most part it follows the edge of Roaring Run Valley. In late May look for jack-in-the-pulpits along here. At 4.5 miles (7.3 km) the trail swings away from the edge and soon picks up an old woods road. As the old road becomes more distinct, you bear left on a still more prominent road. Shortly you turn right on a fainter road and descend to a crossing of a dry water course. Immediately beyond, turn right on another woods road. This road traverses the steep north slope of Birch Rock Hill and, when the leaves are off, should provide some views north across the Roaring Run Valley to Painter Rock Hill beyond. At 6.2 miles (10 km) turn the corner of Birch Rock Hill and pass the signed Birch Rock side trail that leads to Birch Rock overlook near the edge of the state forest land. If the day is clear, this would make a good side trip. For the most part, the blue-blazed side trail follows old woods roads. But just before reaching Birch Rock, the trail diverges to the left. If you miss this turn, you will reach some houses at the end of a road on private land. Retrace your steps to the South Loop trail.

Just 20 yards beyond bear right on the South Loop Trail. The trail now descends steadily. Soon another old road comes in from the left and at 6.9

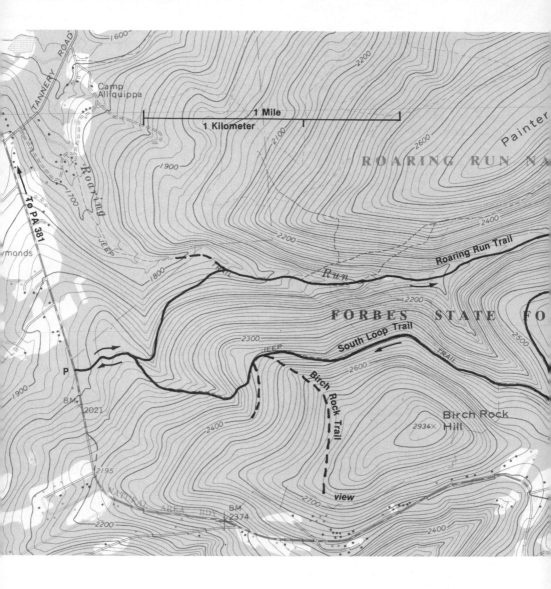

miles (11.1 km) you turn left on the trail on which you came in. In 0.3 miles (500 m) you are back to the County Line Road and your car.

Other opportunities for hiking the Roaring Run Natural Area are the North Loop and Painter Rock trails, which form a large circuit, and the Laurel Highlands Trail, which crosses the southeastern corner of the area.

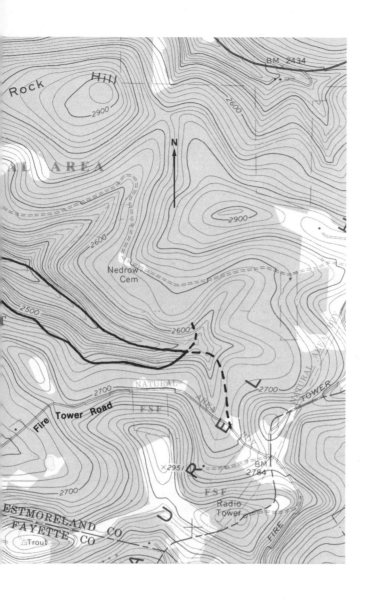

Rock Hill

BM 2434

2600

2900

2900

N

AL AREA

2600

Nedrow
Cem

2500

2600

2700

NATURAL

AREA

2700

Fire Tower Road

FSF

2700

TOWER

NATURAL AREA

×295

R

BM
2784

FSF

2700

Radio
Tower

FIRE

ESTMORELAND
FAYETTE CO.
CO.

△Trout

10

Laurel Hill State Park

Distance: 7.7 miles (12.4 km)
Time: 4½ hours
Rise: 760 feet (230 m)
Highlight: Old-growth hemlock
Maps: USGS 7½' Bakersville, Seven Springs,
    Rockwood; state park map

Laurel Hill State Park, in Somerset County, ranks as one of the larger parks in western Pennsylvania, having almost 4,000 acres. Back in the 1930s, Laurel Hill was one of five federal demonstration parks in Pennsylvania. The others were Raccoon, Blue Knob, Hickory Run and French Creek. After World War II these parks were transferred to the Commonwealth, with the stipulation that they continue to be used for recreation. Two of the nine group camps at Laurel Hill were once Civilian Conservation Corps camps. Do not confuse Laurel Hill State Park, which is in Laurel Hill Creek valley, with Laurel Ridge State Park, which is on top of the hill, or with Laurel Mountain State Park, which is a downhill ski area north of the Turnpike.

Laurel Hill State Park can be reached from PA 31, just east of Bakersville, by traveling south on LR (Legislative Route) 55052 for 1.7 miles to the eastern park entrance. The park can also be reached from PA 281 at New Centerville by driving west on LR 55049 for about 4 miles to the southern park entrance, just beyond an Exxon station and Red and White food store. This hike starts from the beach parking area, which is on the main park road connecting these two entrances, 0.7 mile from the south entrance, and 2.8 miles from the east entrance.

Begin the hike by heading north along the park road. At the first road junction bear left on the road to group camp 8 and go around the vehicle gate. To the left of where this road enters the woods, there are some graves, which predate the park. At the far end of the group camp, continue straight ahead into the woods on a snowmobile trail. The ridge trail comes up from the right at 0.5 mile (0.8 km), and soon the aqueduct diverges to the right. Trails in this park are usually not signed. Soon a trail comes in from the left, and at 0.8 mile (1.2 km) you bear right and descend gently to Jones Mill Run. At 1.1 miles (1.7 km) you cross the run on a snowmobile bridge and turn left on the Tram Road Trail. This is the route of a logging railroad, operated by the United Lumber Company, that hauled logs to a sawmill at Humbert, near the confluence of Laurel Hill Creek and the Casselman River.

Next you come to a crossing of Jones Mill Run. If the water is high, you can avoid this crossing by bearing right, because the Tram Road Trail soon returns to this side. Farther upstream there is another crossing that could also be avoided the same way, since the Tram Road Trail recrosses the run opposite the ruins of the old pump house and just below the small dam.

The pond behind the dam is a popular spot with fishermen. Avoid the trail fishermen have worn along the edge of the pond. Instead keep left on the Tram Road Trail where the Pump House Trail joins it from the right. Farther along, turn right at an obscure junction where the Tram Road Trail diverges to the left. At 2.3 miles (3.7 km) you cross the aqueduct and immediately turn left on the Martz Trail.

At 2.5 miles (4.0 km) the Martz Trail meets the Beltz Road Trail, which forms

Jones Mill Run Dam

the border between Laurel Hill State Park and Forbes State Forest. This hillside has recently been clear-cut. Turn right and you soon leave the clear-cut behind. The yellow spots on the trees along the Beltz Trail indicate the trees that are to be saved. At 2.8 miles (4.4 km) turn right on the Bobcat Trail. This junction is obscure; the only marker is a sign post that has been split by vandals who removed the sign. If you miss this turn, you will cross a stream and come to the corner of a selective cut farther along the Beltz Trail, followed by a snowmobile trail to the left and a sign for Kooser State Park.

The Bobcat Trail is easy to follow with its well defined footway and occasional yellow blazes. At 3.1 miles (5.0 km) you cross Buck Run. Shortly beyond the crossing, there is a spring to the right of the trail. Farther on, the trail parallels Buck Run, eventually crossing a large but nameless tributary. At 3.9 miles (6.3 km) you turn left on Buck Run Road and soon pass the Boy Scout Buck Run High Adventure Camp. You turn right at 4.1 miles (6.6 km) on the obvious but unmarked Hemlock Trail, cross Buck Run and bear left at a fork in the trail.

The four acres of virgin hemlock are found at 4.3 miles (6.9 km). As usual with small patches of old-growth trees in Penns Woods, the manner of their survival is not known. If a logger cut his neighbor's timber, he had to pay triple damages. So unless he had complete confidence in his surveyor, he was better off leaving uncut any small tracts of doubtful ownership. Perhaps these four acres are another monument to poor surveying.

The trail continues along a secluded section of Laurel Hill Creek. At 4.9 miles (7.9 km) you turn left on the paved park road, cross the bridge over

Laurel Hill Creek, and then turn right on the Lake Trail. This is your last chance to shorten this hike by walking back along the park road. An old trailside shelter soon appears on the slope above the lake. This shelter was built of chestnut logs by the Civilian Conservation Corps before World War II. There are a few holes in the roof, but if you reach it in a summer thunderstorm, as I did, it is a very welcome refuge. Farther along is a piped spring. However, camping is not permitted here because there is no toilet.

The Lake Trail continues along the steep east side of Laurel Hill Lake, sometimes it follows almost at the water's edge, but often climbing far up the slope. At 6.2 miles (9.9 km) you reach the spillway, but there is no bridge across the creek here. The Lake Trail soon enters a meadow and then crosses a dilapidated bridge over a side stream. The trail skirts the edge of private land to emerge on the paved road L.R. 55049 at 6.8 miles (10.9 km). Turn right past the gas station and food store, cross the bridge over Laurel Hill Creek and immediately turn right again on a fishermen's trail. This trail is informal and unmaintained, but it goes all the way to the base of the dam. (Most fishermen's trails only go as far as the first place the fish bite.) Along the way you will see spruce and white pine in an evergreen plantation, large white oaks, ironwood, beech, serviceberry, red oak, rhododendron, azalea and perhaps even a fisherman. When you reach the dam, cut left along the base, and make your way behind the beach to the concession stand. Turn left, and you are soon back in the beach parking area where you left your car.

A longer hike to Kooser Fire Tower on the Laurel Highlands Hiking Trail from Laurel Hill State Park is described in Hike 13.

11

Quebec Run Wild Area

Distance: 8.1 miles (13.0 km)
Time: 4½ hours
Rise: 1,040 feet (315 m)
Highlights: Abandoned gold mine;
  mountain streams
Maps: USGS 7½' Bruceton Mills, Brownfield;
  State Forest Wild Area map

The Quebec Run Wild Area is a heavily forested section of land in Forbes State Forest on the eastern slope of Chestnut Ridge, just a bit north of the Mason-Dixon Line. Chestnut Ridge, like Laurel Ridge, is an anticline. Layers of rock have been gently folded to form a great arch. It helps to have the topmost layer a hard one, resistant to erosion. The hard upper layer of Chestnut Ridge is Pottsville sandstone. This stone is of great significance in Pennsylvania, because all the commercial coal seams lie above it. There are a few traces of Devonian coal below, but they are of interest primarily to geologists. Quebec Run Wild Area also contains Pennsylvania's only gold mine. Unlike the quartz vein deposits found in the west, this mine is a placer deposit, formed when the streams that deposited the Pottsville sandstone eroded through a quartz vein in the long-gone mountains to the east of Pennsylvania 230 million years ago.

The trailhead for Quebec Run Wild Area is most easily reached from US 40 east of Uniontown. Turn south at the top of Chestnut Ridge on the Seaton Road, just east of the Mount Summit Inn. Follow the signs for Laurel Caverns, but continue past the cavern turnoff. Bypass the road to Pondfield Fire Tower (which, by the way, commands a splendid view of Chestnut Ridge). At 6.5 miles from US 40, turn left on the Mud Pike (no sign but well named) for 1.3 miles more to the parking lot at the north end of the gated Quebec Road.

The hike starts off from the parking lot on the blue-blazed Miller Trail, which descends gently along a ridge between Mill Run and a nameless tributary to the west. Chestnut Ridge was named for the American chestnut tree, which sprouts abundantly along this trail. The chestnut was a versatile tree; in town its spreading branches provided shade, while in the forest it grew straight and tall for timber. Its beautiful wood was suitable for both rough and fine construction, and since it resisted rot, it was used for fence posts, too. When the tree was cut, the stump would resprout vigorously. The nuts provided

View East from Chestnut Ridge

food for both wildlife and man. At the turn of the century the American chestnut comprised about half of the wood in the Appalachians from Maine to Georgia. These forests were decimated by a fungal blight *(Endothia parasitica)* which killed the above-ground portion of the trees. The roots were not affected, however; and today, some eighty years later, they continue to send up healthy shoots. Although some of these shoots grow large enough to bear nuts, they eventually contract the blight and die. Recently, though, a viral parasite that weakens *Endothia parasitica* was introduced. Perhaps, at long last, the tide

is about to turn, and the American chestnut may once again cover the many flats, ridges and hollows that now bear only its name and a few stumps where life continues to smoulder underground.

You pass a mini-view up Mill Run at 0.9 mile (1.4 km), and then you cross the nameless tributary on stepping stones. The stream flows through a rhododendron thicket. A little farther along, the trail follows an old logging railroad grade.

Look for deer tracks in the mud. I found two sets, one full-sized, the other diminutive. Evidently they were from a doe and her fawn. The tracks were so fresh and sharp that I suspect the deer were moving down the trail ahead of me, just far enough ahead to keep out of sight.

At 1.3 miles (2.1 km) bear left on the Mill Run Trail at the junction with the Rankin Trail. The Miller Trail ends here. As in Roaring Run Natural Area, trail signs are spiked to the trees. Shortly you must cross Quebec Run itself. It is too wide to jump, but a pile of logs a bit downstream served as a somewhat slippery bridge for me. In slightly lower water, you should be able to use the stepping stones.

Next, you reach the edge of Mill Run itself, a formidable stream. The map of the wild area indicates the ruins of a grist mill are to be found on the far side of Mill Run. If the run is low enough or warm enough, you could cross over and hunt for them. The Mill Run Trail continues downstream, sometimes right along Mill Run, and at other times out of sight of the stream. The old railroad grade is used whenever it is on the west side, but frequently it is on the east side. You cross many sidestreams, some small and some rather large, before you turn right at 2.9 miles (4.6 km) and start the long climb back up

the flank of Chestnut Ridge. It soon becomes evident that you are following the old West Road. At 3.0 miles (4.8 km) you turn left on the Tebolt Trail and continue to climb, but more gently, as you follow it through a small meadow.

You reach the Brocker Trail at 3.2 miles (5.1 km) and turn right on it through a stand of larch or tamarack. At 3.6 miles (5.7 km) you cross an old road that leads south to the edge of the Wild Area along Wirsing Road. Continue ahead on the Brocker Trail, crossing a ravine and the traces of several old logging roads, to the Quebec Road at 4.5 miles (7.2 km). Cross the Quebec Road and continue on the unblazed but obvious West Road which climbs the side of Chestnut Ridge.

At 5.2 miles (8.3 km) look sharp for the Hess Trail, just before the rhododendrons close in across the West Road. A sign for the Hess Trail is spiked to a tree. Turn right on the Hess Trail which takes you downhill on an old road along a stream. You cross this stream and then another one before descending into the valley of Quebec Run itself, which you cross at 6.5 miles (10.4 km). Immediately up the bank, you turn left on the Rankin Trail and follow it around the bend to where the Hess Trail turns right uphill. At the top of the hill the old gold mine diggings appear to the right of the trail, and just beyond there is a view to the east. You cross a stream and continue climbing. At 7.8 miles (12.4 km) you cross an old road and continue to the parking lot.

Backpacking is permitted in the Quebec Run Wild Area, but you should obtain a camping permit from the district forest office in Ligonier. The Rankin Trail, Tebolt Trail, and Quebec Road provide alternatives that could be used to either lengthen or shorten this hike. Or you could visit Laurel Caverns for a cool hike underground.

12

Bear Run Nature Reserve

Distance: 8.8 miles (14.3 km)
Time: 5¼ hours
Rise: 1,160 feet (355 meters)
Highlights: Wild flowers, mountain streams,
  views
Maps: USGS 7½' Mill Run; Bear Run Trail Map
  (Frequently available at trailhead, and from
  Western Pennsylvania Conservancy)

Normally, the Western Pennsylvania Conservancy transfers acquired lands to public ownership. There is one area, however, that the Conservancy chose to keep. This is the Bear Run Nature Reserve. The Conservancy has expanded the original tract surrounding Fallingwater, Frank Lloyd Wright's famous house, to 3,500 acres. The Reserve stretches from the banks of the Youghiogheny far up the western flank of Laurel Hill and encompasses most of the watersheds of both Laurel Run and Bear Run itself. Almost 20 miles of trails lace the reserve, which is open to nonmembers for both day hiking and overnight camping. Users of the backpack campsites should register at the parking lot. Reservations are required for the one group campsite (10 or more campers).

This hike takes you on a grand tour of the trails at Bear Run, through dense woods, pine plantations, and rhododendron thickets, across fields and along mountain streams to a view of rafts and kayaks knocking the rocks out of the lower Yough.

The many rocks and wet areas call for hiking boots. There are several ways this hike can be shortened.

Bear Run Nature Reserve is on PA 381 about 4 miles north of Ohiopyle and 3.5 miles south of Mill Run. Drive in at the sign and park in the large lot behind the nature center. The hike begins at the far end of the parking lot.

Head into the pine plantation on the Wagon Trail. Almost immediately the Pine Trail takes off to the left, and very shortly the Arbutus Trail diverges to the right. In theory the Wagon Trail is blazed with orange rectangles, but the trail is wide and well used and the blazing correspondingly scarce. Next, the Poetry Trail goes off to your right. The white pine trees along the Wagon Trail give over now to red pine. After the Aspen Trail, which goes left, you come to spruce.

At 0.5 mile (0.8 km) the Wagon Trail comes to an end and you turn left on the Ridge Trail blazed with yellow spots. Rhododendron thickets, and white oaks border the trail at this point. Shortly, you cross a bridge over Beaver Run and the Arbutus Trail comes in from the right. Listen for the song of the wood-thrush. Next, the white-blazed Rhododendron Trail goes off to the left. (One way to shorten this hike and avoid over 300 feet of climbing would be to take the Rhododendron and Snowbunny trails to the junction of the Laurel Run and Tulip Tree trails.) At 0.6 mile (1.0 km) the Hemlock Trail goes off to the right. Other trees found along this section are red oak, tulip, black gum, chestnut oak, cucumber, black birch, red maple, and the much smaller striped maple. At 1.1 miles (1.7 km) bear left where the Hemlock Trail comes back in from the right, and left again at 1.2 miles (1.9 km) where the old road goes straight ahead.

Teaberry Trail comes in from the left at 1.3 miles (2.0 km). Along this section you can see sassafrass and beech trees as well as mountain laurel. Backpack campsite 2 is found at 2.1 miles (3.4 km) where the Hickory Trail diverges to the right. At 2.4 miles (3.8 km) you reach a junction with the Rhododendron, Bear Run, and Tulip Tree trails. Continue straight ahead on the Tulip Tree Trail, which is also blazed with yellow spots. In late May, look for the pink lady's-slipper. At 2.6 miles (4.1 km) watch the blazes as the Tulip Tree makes an obscure jog to the left near some large rocks. For the most part, the Tulip Tree Trail is fairly faint and re-quires careful attention, particularly at junctions with other old woods roads. Soon the trail begins descending, and at 3.5 miles (5.6 km) you reach the junc-tion with the Snowbunny Trail. This is your last chance to return to the park-ing lot without going around the large inholding of private land or walking back on the highway. Continue ahead on the white-blazed Laurel Trail, and another 0.25 mile (0.4 km) brings you to a cross-ing of Laurel Run itself. A well-traveled

jeep road comes in just beyond the run, and you follow along it until you reach the edge of a field. Turn left and pick up an old woods road that takes you down to PA 381 at 4.4 miles (7.0 km).

Jog right across the highway and continue downhill on another old woods road that closely follows an old barbed wire fence. In places the trail goes through areas that are just plain liquid, but the Laurel Trail is scheduled to be repaired in the near future. By the time you hike it, these boggy sections may have been bridged or bypassed, the several climbs over the barbed wire fence eliminated, and the crossings of Laurel Run reduced to the one shown on the trail map. This crossing should be at about 5.1 miles (8.2 km). At 5.4 miles (8.7 km) after crossing a jeep road, the Laurel Trail pulls away from the run. The trail is obscure in the vicinity of an old coal mine, but on the far side it picks up a fine old road and stays on it.

At about 5.6 miles (9.0 km) the Laurel Run Trail emerges into the lower Yough Gorge and swings upstream, still follow-ing the old road far above the river. At 5.9 miles (9.5 km) you reach a junction with the orange-blazed Saddle Trail which, if you took it, would shorten your hike but would also bypass the overlook of the Yough at the west end of the peninsula.

In another 0.2 mile (0.3 km) you pass campsite no. 4 to the right of the trail.

At 6.6 miles (10.6 km) the trail picks up a pole line. Although this is out in the open, a considerable amount of brush makes the trail obscure. At times the trail follows an old quarry above the pole line, but this isn't much better. There is even some poison ivy to keep things interesting, and this next kilometer is a long one. At 7.3 miles (11.6 km) however, you emerge at an overlook that makes it all worthwhile.

You are 20 meters directly above the main line of the Baltimore and Ohio Railroad. You get a good view of the river at Dimple Rapids and can watch the kayaks and rafts dodging the many rocks. You probably heard the screams and shouts from below as you hiked the Peninsula Trail, but now you can actually see what is going on.

Back on the Peninsula Trail you traverse the slope for the next 0.6 mile (0.9 km) without benefit of old grades. At 7.8 miles (12.4 km) you reach a side trail to another overlook. Although this overlook is at the brink of an impressive cliff you can't see the river when the leaves are out. Continuing on the Peninsula, you climb to the edge of a field where you turn right. The trail then enters a patch of woods at the far end of which the Saddle Trail comes in from the left. The wooded area gives out onto another field with views to the east of Laurel Hill. If the sun is too hot, you can vary the walk back by turning left on the yellow-blazed Kinglet Trail. In either case, it is about 0.5 mile (0.8 km) back to PA 381, just across from the entrance to the Bear Run parking lot.

As this hike uses less than half the trails in Bear Run Nature Reserve, there are plenty of opportunities for further hiking. As mentioned earlier, Fallingwater, the famous house designed by Frank Lloyd Wright, is near at hand, and well worth a visit.

To reach Fallingwater, turn south on PA 381 for half a mile and then turn right at the sign.

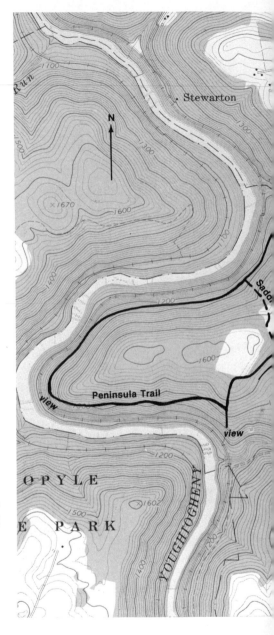

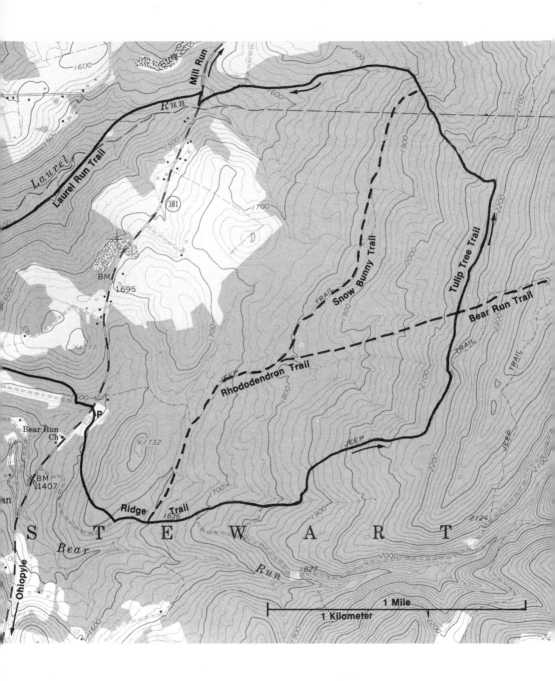

13

Kooser Fire Tower

Distance: 10.4 miles (16.7 km)
Time: 6 hours
Rise: 1,480 feet (450 m)
Highlights: Views, Laurel Highlands Trail
Maps: USGS 7½' Seven Springs, Bakersville;
    State Forest Ski Touring and Snowmobile
    Trail map*

When the state forests were first established, forest fires often raged through the slash left by the loggers. To help fight these fires, the state built a system of fire towers. These towers provided some of the best views in Penn's Woods. In recent years, however, small airplanes with infrared detectors have taken over the search for forest fires. The infrared detectors are more sensitive than human lookouts, although if the fire is at the end of the plane's search pattern, it may get a good start before it is detected. Thus, many fire towers are being torn down, and the views can rarely, if ever, be duplicated from the ground. When I visited Kooser Fire Tower, it was no longer used, but there were no plans to tear it down.

The trailhead for this hike is on the Buck Run road in Laurel Hill State Park. See Hike 10 for directions to this park. Buck Run road leaves the main park road 1.7 miles from the south entrance and 1.8 miles from the east entrance. This junction is marked with a sign for

group camps 4 and 6. Follow the Buck Run road for 0.6 mile to a small parking lot on your right. The Martz Trail begins on the gated road directly opposite this lot. Most of the trails followed on this hike are used by snowmobiles in the winter and are thus closed to hikers during snow season. Owing to the length of this hike, boots are strongly recommended.

Head up the Martz Trail, step around the vehicle gate, ignore a road to the right, and cross the Water Line Trail. At 0.6 mile (0.9 km) continue straight past a clearing, and then keep right where the aqueduct continues ahead. At 1.1 miles (1.8 km) the Pump House Trail comes in from the left, and at 1.3 miles (2.1 km) you turn right on the Beltz Trail along the edge of a large clearcut in Forbes State Forest.

As you move up the Beltz Trail, which forms the boundary between Forbes State Forest and Laurel Hill State Park, you leave the clearcut behind and pass the obscure junction with the Bobcat

*Available from Forbes State Forest, 132 West Main St., Ligonier, PA 15658.

Kooser Fire Tower

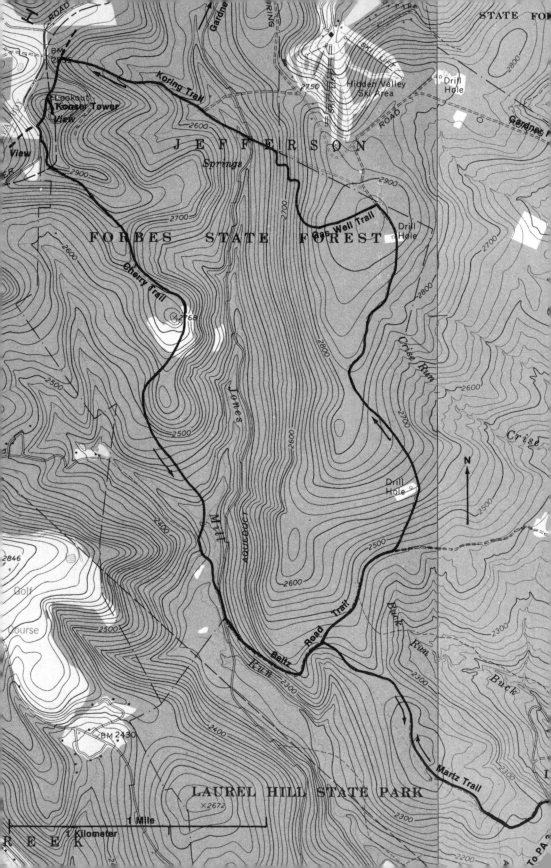

Trail. Next you cross the headwaters of Buck Run and come to the edge of a selective logging cut on your left. At 1.8 miles (2.9 km) you turn left on a logging road leading uphill. A sign indicates this is the way to Kooser State Park. There is an open area at 2.1 miles (3.4 km) which was the site of a well drilled for natural gas. The lack of any wellhead installation suggests it was a dry hole. Bear right at this clearing to pick up the trail again. Although the USGS map indicates that the trail next crosses private land, Forbes State Forest has been expanded here making the entire trail state owned. When the selective cut ends, continue through the woods to the top of the hill. You then go through and along some older clearcuts, which are full of bird life. Listen for the catbird's meow and the towhee's "drink your tea".

At 3.3 miles (5.2 km) you enter a clearing that was probably the site of another unproductive gas well. A giant microwave tower punctures the sky above you. Continue across the clearing and turn left on the access road to the microwave tower. At the far side, beyond a black metal tank, pick up the Gas Well Trail which bears left into the woods, away from the guy wires for the tower. At the far side of the old clearcut, you start the descent towards Jones Mill Run. Partway down the hill, you enter a selective cut, and the trail switches back and forth on the steep slope. Kooser Tower can be seen rising above the trees on the next ridge. The Koring Trail, actually a pipe line swath, is found at 4.3 miles (6.8 km) at a corner of state forest land. Turn left on the Koring Trail and follow it downhill, crossing the Jones Mill Run road, and then the run itself, which is quite small at this point.

Now you start to climb the main ridge of Laurel Hill. As you continue to climb, the Gas Well Trail rejoins Koring Trail. Next you reach the edge of a clearcut on the left. The far edge is your landmark to look sharp for the Laurel Highlands Trail crossing, just 300 feet farther. There is a sign, but it is back in the trees on the right. You turn left on the Laurel Highlands Trail as it climbs gently through an old spruce and red pine plantation. At 5.3 miles (8.5 km) you cross the road leading to Kooser Fire Tower, but there is a shorter route just ahead where the trail passes under a pole line. (If the tower has been torn down, you can get a view east and north by following the access road left about 300 feet.) Turn left and follow a faint footway along the pole line up the slope, emerging in the clearing next to a woodshed. The tower is at the far side of the clearing. Do not attempt to climb the tower if the lower steps have been removed; but if the tower is intact, the views from the top are panoramic. Laurel Hill and Seven Springs Ski Area can be seen to the south; to the west is Roaring Run Natural Area, and on a clear day you can also see Chestnut Ridge. The southeast affords a view of Negro Mountain, topped by Mt. Davis (Hike 5), and due east the microwave tower crowns the ridge you just climbed. This ridge is being intensively managed for timber production. The fire tower cabin is not open to the public.

Back on the ground, retrace your steps to the Laurel Highlands Trail and turn left. At 5.8 miles (9.3 km) you reach the Tower road. If you follow the Laurel Highlands Trail ahead into a small meadow, you can get another view over Roaring Run Natural Area. To continue this hike, bear left on the Tower road, then bear left again on a gated road, just across from the Roaring Run Natural Area sign. This is the Cherry Trail, named for the black cherry, as you will see. On the Cherry

Trail, you soon enter an old clearcut, and then pass through a clearing for wildlife food. A mature forest offers little for wildlife to eat, and such openings are deliberate attempts to improve the habitat. Until the new forest surrounding this clearing grows up, there is a view of the ridge on the far side of Jones Mill Run. The Cherry Trail traverses the clearcut and continues in the woods on the far side. Black cherry trees are common here. Keep right where an old road goes straight ahead, and at 8.1 miles (12.9 km) cross a stream on the snowmobile bridge and climb the bank on the far side. At the top, turn left on the Beltz Road Trail ignoring the road to the right at a spruce planting. Soon you come out along Jones Mill Run, which is now a much larger stream than where you crossed it before. This time your crossing is on a steel bridge, and beyond it, at 8.4 miles (13.5 km), you bear right on the Jones Mill Run road. Soon you bear left on the Beltz Road Trail again and climb past the extensive clearcut on your left. At 9.1 miles (14.5 km) you reach a junction with the Martz Trail. A trail sign indicates the way to Laurel Hill State Park. This is the point where you joined the Beltz Trail earlier. Turn right on the Martz Trail and retrace your steps to your car.

14

Maple Summit To Ohiopyle

Distance: 11.3 miles (18.0 km)
Time: 6½ hours
Rise: 1,700 feet (520 m)
Highlight: Views
Maps: USGS 7½' Mill Run, Ohiopyle;
   Hikers Guide to Laurel Highlands,
   maps 1 and 2; Laurel Ridge State Park map

Laurel Ridge is a giant arch of gently folded rock, an anticline. Like Chestnut Ridge, its cap is composed of a layer of hard Pottsville sandstone which resists erosion. This sandstone lies under the Ohiopyle waterfall, then rises gently upwards—about 1,700 feet—to form Laurel Ridge. This is a modest anticline compared to some in the ridge-and-valley region to the east which appear to have exceeded 30,000 feet. But Laurel Ridge has survived more or less intact, whereas the ridge-and-valley anticlines have been leveled by erosion.

The Youghiogheny River has cut a water gap through Laurel Ridge, making this southermost section of the Laurel Highlands Trail one of the most scenic. For much of its length the top of Laurel Ridge is broad and relatively flat, making views and overlooks rare. The section between Ohiopyle and Maple Summit also contains one of the longest climbs on the Laurel Highlands Trail. While this hike is arranged so that you go down hill, the north flank of Youghiogheny Gorge still requires several steep climbs.

To do this hike you need a car shuttle, or preferably a drop-off service. At the time of this writing, however, none of the outfitters at Ohiopyle was interested in providing this service for hikers. If that is still so, you must either make your own drop-off arrangements or use a car shuttle. Leave one car in a lot in Ohiopyle and drive north on PA 381 in the other car. At 1.9 miles north of the bridge, turn right and drive up the flank of Laurel Ridge. After 4.0 miles more, turn right again. It is another 1.8 miles to the obscure trail crossing. There is no parking at the crossing, but there is a game commission parking lot on the left, just 0.1 mile farther, and there is a side trail to the Laurel Highlands Trail from the lot. Overnight parking is not permitted at the game commission lot. There are shelters on this section of the trail, so this hike could be turned into a two-day backpack, if you can make drop-off arrangements. Whether you do this as a day hike or as a backpack, hiking boots are strongly recommended.

As you head south along the yellow-blazed Laurel Highlands Trail, the first landmark you see is milepost 11 at 0.4 mile (0.6 km) from the Maple Summit Road. Despite the substantial split log bridges at the many wet spots there is still a good deal of water on this section of trail. At 0.9 mile (1.5 km) you cross Little Glade Run and begin a gentle climb towards the western edge of Laurel Hill. After passing some big rocks, you reach milepost 10. Next you pass along the base of a small cliff on your right, and at 1.8 miles (2.8 km) you cross a jeep road in a cleared swath. This road appears to service several natural gas wells. Anticlines like Laurel Ridge are textbook traps for oil and gas. Alex Run is crossed at 2.3 miles (3.7 km), and shortly you reach milepost 9. Next you approach the edge of Laurel Ridge where the guide book indicates a view to the west. On my hike, the fog was so thick that I missed it.

The trail continues close to the western edge, past milepost 8. At 3.9 miles (6.2 km) there are several obvious side trails out to more views. Every time I've hiked this section, fog has prevented me from seeing these views as well. Soon you start down the great descent into the Youghiogheny Gorge. Twice you cross another jeep road that leads to some natural gas wells. At 4.4 miles (7.0 km) you bear right on an old road and pass milepost 7. There is a view over Camp Run Ravine as you continue to descend. Shortly you pass a white-blazed boundary between State Game Land No. 111 and Ohiopyle State Park.

A side trail goes left to the Camp Run shelters at 5.0 miles (8.1 km). If you've never seen a Laurel Highlands Trail shelter, take the time to inspect one. The built-in fireplace gives lots of heat. There is a well here for drinking water and also pit toilets, including one for the handicapped.

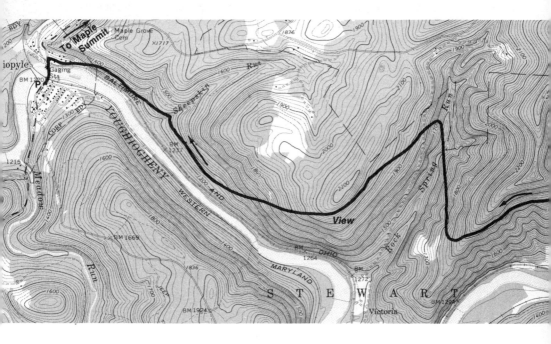

Trail Shelter

Back on the Laurel Highlands Trail, at the bottom of the great descent there is a meadow with some poison ivy. At 5.3 miles (8.5 km) you cross a jeep road and Lick Run and then come to milepost 6. The trail continues in and out of meadows to 5.9 miles (9.5 km) where you cross a nameless stream. This is followed by a good stiff climb that continues past milepost 5. You follow along the hillside high above the Yough with occasional views of the other side of the gorge. At 7.4 miles (11.8 km) you come to milepost 4, above the large bend in the Yough that encloses the Flats. There is a fair amount of open meadow along this section. At 7.8 miles (12.5 km) you cross Rock Spring Run and begin another climb that continues almost to milepost 3.

The Laurel Highlands Trail has saved the best for the last. At 9.1 miles (14.5 km) you come to the edge of cliffs with spectacular views of the Yough and spectacular drops to the rocks below. Be careful. There are no guard rails. From here the trail leads downward until it is just above the Baltimore and Ohio tracks. A giant boulder is passed at 10.3 miles (16.5 km), then milepost 1. Next, you cross Sheepskin Run and then another run. A trail at 10.8 miles (17.2 km) leads right to the hiker parking lot.

Shortly the Laurel Highlands Trail bears left off an old road, descends, and turns right on to the jeep road along the Baltimore and Ohio tracks. Please sign the trail register. Maintenance of the Laurel Highlands Trail depends on the level of usage. Continue into the outskirts of Ohiopyle, and 11.3 miles (18.0 km) brings you to PA 381.

There are other hikes at Ohiopyle State Park and nearby Bear Run Nature Reserve. See Hikes 1, 6, 12 and 15.

15

Baughman's Rock

Distance: 12 miles (19.4 km)
Time: 6½ hours
Rise: 1,100 feet (335 meters)
Highlight: Views of Youghiogheny River
Maps: USGS 7½' Ohiopyle; state park map

This hike is a real bootbuster and should definitely not be your first hike. It takes you up the steep southern side of the Youghiogheny Gorge to a natural overlook called Baughman's (pronounced Bachman's) Rock, then down a dead-end and little-used jeep road to the bed of the abandoned Western Maryland Railroad. Despite its length, the entire hike is within the borders of Ohiopyle State Park.

Of the nearly 19,000 acres of Ohiopyle State Park, over 5,000 were obtained through the Western Pennsylvania Conservancy. The Western Maryland Railroad donated over 60 miles of abandoned right-of-way along the Yough. This hike uses part of a 27 mile stretch that is to be developed into a hiking/biking trail. Rocks and wet spots call for hiking boots, and there is poison ivy along the trail.

This hike begins right in the village of Ohiopyle. From PA 381 turn east next to the Falls Market (formerly Holt's Department Store) and park in the lot just beyond the old Western Maryland Railroad station. You can drive about a quarter mile (400 meters) down the old grade to the parking lot at the Middle Yough takeout, but this lot is rather isolated. It is mostly used, for takeout well above the falls, by people canoeing the Yough from Confluence to Ohiopyle.

At the far end of the takeout parking lot is a vehicle gate blocking the railroad grade. The Baughman Trail begins here and climbs away from the railroad. The trail is marked with red paint blazes. After a particularly steep pitch you reach an old road which comes from the end of the street in Ohiopyle. Turn left and continue climbing at a more gradual rate. At 0.8 mile (1.3 km) you bear right on another old road. Three more old roads to the left are passed as you continue to climb. The trail levels off briefly at 1.6 miles (2.5 km) but climbs again by the time you reach a small clearing. Here the trail makes an obscure turn to the left. The trail soon enters another clearing with a good stand of poison ivy, so watch your step. Along this stretch the trail is also marked with painted arrows. Watch for the interrupted fern, which has a cluster of spore cases part way up the frond.

Soon the trail comes within sight of the road (LR 26116) and at 2.3 miles (3.7 km) you arrive at the parking lot for Baughman Rock. Turn left for a vista of

Baughman Hollow, the Flats inside the bend in the Youghiogheny, and Laurel Ridge beyond.

Picking up the trail again, you continue through the formation of large rocks of which Baughman Rock is a part. The road slowly forces the trail over the edge to descend a little below the rim where it continues on a succession of old roads.

Sometimes in such thick vegetation, you may hear a large animal go crashing through the brush. It comes to a halt, still entirely out of sight. Now you hear a succession of snorts, perhaps accompanied by hoof stomps. What is it? A bear? A wild boar? No, it's just a deer. If the deer hears you, but doesn't get wind of you, it can't figure out what you are. It's hard to believe that deer can make such undeerlike noises, but they do.

You cross Long Run on a split log bridge and then climb back to the paved road, where you emerge at an unsigned junction at 3.4 miles (5.4 km). Turn left along the paved road for about 300 yards to another unsigned junction with a jeep road. The jeep road leads to a couple of natural gas wells down near the river and carries no through traffic. It is mostly in the shade and so makes a fairly pleasant hike. The road leads generally down with occasional views of

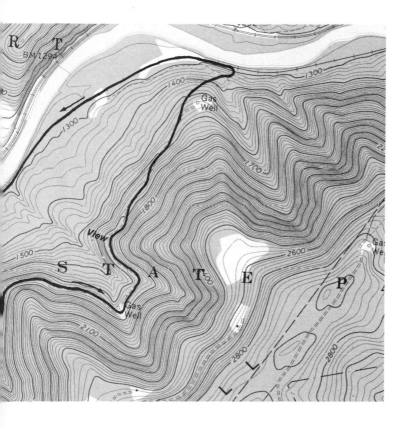

the valley below. In muddy places look for the cloven footprints of deer. After descending for two kilometers, the jeep road slowly reclimbs part of the mountainside to ford a nameless stream. It then gives a view down the valley of the Yough before reaching a gas well at 6.1 miles (9.8 km). Continue across the clearing and at 7.0 miles (11.3 km) bear left at a steel vehicle gate before reaching a second gas well. Small deposits of natural gas are widely distributed in western Pennsylvania.

This old road descends steadily and soon crosses a small stream at an uprooted vehicle gate. You next reach the bottom of the hill, and shortly you can see the Western Maryland Railroad grade through the trees. As soon as you see the railroad grade, cut through the woods to it. There isn't any connecting trail, but it's only about 50 yards. When you hit the railroad grade, turn left. There are occasional glimpses of the river, but mostly it remains out of sight behind the trees. At 7.9 miles (12.6 km) you see a track leading right. It is apparently used by fishermen for access to the river.

Returning to the railroad, the next landmark you see is a meadow to the left containing the ruins of a building. The railroad grade crosses a number of streams. They are hard to see through the dense vegetation, but you can hear them splashing down the hillside. At 8.9 miles (14.4 km) you cross one of the largest of them. It is the unnamed stream you forded back up on the jeep road. Next, cliffs covered with rhododendrons encroach on the railroad grade, and the river is constantly in view. You are rounding the large bend around the Flats on the north side of the Yough.

At 9.6 miles (15.4 km) you cross a bridge over another side stream with a mini-waterfall. This is Long Run, which you crossed far up near the edge of the gorge. The railroad grade, which was covered with loose gravel ballast where you met it, has gradually become firmer and easier for walking. The vehicle gate is reached at 11.8 miles (19 km), and a further quarter mile returns you to your car at the old railroad station.

There are further hiking opportunities in Ohiopyle State Park. See Hikes 1, 6 and 14. In addition, there is a small network of trails along Meadow Run just north of the park office that are known for spring wild flowers.

16

State Game Lands 42

Distance: 13.5 miles (21.9 km)
Time: 7 hours
Rise: 1,840 feet (560 m)
Highlights: Laurel Highlands Trail, mountain
    streams, signs of bears and deer
Maps: USGS 7½' Rachel Wood; Hiker's Guide to
    Laurel Highlands Trail, maps 10 and 11

In the western part of the state there are over 250,000 acres of state game land. Next to Allegheny National Forest, these are the most abundant of all public lands. Yet they have few marked trails. The Laurel Highlands Trail traverses game lands 111 and 42, while the Baker Trail passes through game lands 24, 283 and 74. The Pennsylvania Game Commission buys several thousand acres of new game lands every year. But as the commission is supported mainly by hunting license fees, you can understand why it tries to serve hunters rather than hikers.

This hike takes you on a boot-busting tour of the largest of the four tracts of State Game Lands 42. It uses the Laurel Highlands Trail, snowmobile trails and management roads to make a loop down the west flank of Laurel Hill. It is the longest hike in this book. But the Game Commission prohibits camping on its lands, so you can't turn this hike into a backpack. Neither is there any way to shorten it, except by turning back before you reach the midpoint. Be sure you are in good physical condition and

have recently taken another hike almost as long. You need plenty of daylight, so don't take this hike during the late fall, winter or early spring when darkness comes early. At least be sure you've got a good flashlight with fresh batteries in your pack. You will certainly need your hiking boots.

The trailhead is on PA 271, between Oak Grove and Johnstown. It is the regular parking area for the Laurel Highlands Trail and is 8.3 miles east of the junction with PA 711. As usual, a sign warns that cars are left at the owner's risk. The greatest risk is at night, particulary on weekends. This parking area is located farther from the Laurel Highlands Trail than any other, because of private land ownership along the trail. Head up the blue-blazed side trail. Be sure to sign in at the trail register, even though you are just day hiking. Funds for trail maintenance depend on usage.

You pass the side trail to the shelter area, and at 0.6 mile (1.0 km) you turn right on the yellow-blazed Laurel Highlands Trail. Next you cross PA 271

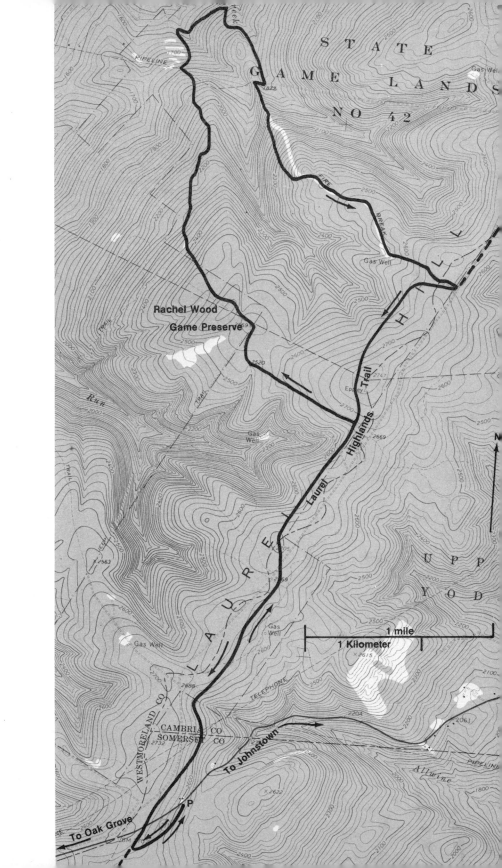

STATE
GAME LANDS
NO 42

Rachel Wood
Game Preserve

FIRE

BREAK

Gas Well

HILL

Highlands Trail

Laurel

L
A
U
R
E
L

UPP

YOD

Rachel Wood
Game Preserve

Gas Well

Gas Well

Gas Well

Gas Well

N

1 mile
1 Kilometer

WESTMORELAND CO
CAMBRIA CO
SOMERSET CO

TELEPHONE

To Johnstown

PIPELINE

Altoona

To Oak Grove

P

(no parking along the highway) and at 0.8 mile (1.2 km) you pass milepost 57. Continue through rather open woods, crossing a pipe line swath and then a telephone line. Somewhere between the telephone line and milepost 58 at 1.8 miles (2.9 km) you enter State Game Lands 42. Next you cross an old woods road and then a swath through the woods. The gravel road you cross at 2.6 miles (4.2 km) is the principal management road for Game Lands 42. Milepost 59 is reached at 2.8 miles (4.5 km).

The trail is often edged with flat rocks, but every once in a while you may find one of these rocks in the middle of the trail. Look at the ground where the rock used to be. If it hasn't rained recently, you may still see the ant tunnels that were underneath. A bear may have turned over this rock in his search for ants and grubs. You may also see rotten logs that have been moved or torn apart by a bear in his search for food.

The trail is crossed by a number of jeep roads leading to gas wells or game food plots. Two jeep roads come in rapid succession at 3.4 miles (5.4 km). These roads tell you that the next one is the one you want. At 3.6 miles (5.7 km) turn left onto a third grassy road. (If you reach milepost 60, you missed the turn.) The grassy road does not lose much elevation at first. Occasional orange diamonds on the trees show it is a snowmobile trail in winter. At 4.4 miles (7.0 km) you round the fenced corner of the Rachel Wood Game Preserve. Like most private land, it is posted. Note the absence of underbrush in the preserve in comparison with the game land. The large deer herd has browsed everything, even the ferns.

Ignore an old road to the left at 4.7 miles (7.5 km), and soon you begin to descend steeply. Near the bottom of the hill, the bedrock itself can be seen. Note its obvious slope here on the flank of Laurel Ridge. At 6.1 miles (9.7 km) jog left across a natural gas pipe line. Beyond, you pass a number of game food plots on the left. Switchback sharply to the right and then cross a bridge over Shannon Run. The creek is bordered with hemlocks and rhododendrons. This is the lowest point on the hike, and it is pretty much all uphill from here. At 6.7 miles (10.7 km) turn right on another snowmobile/management road. Soon you cross Baldwin Creek, which also has large rhododendrons and hemlocks. There is a small waterfall just above the bridge. Jog right across the pipe line swath and cross Baldwin Creek again at 7.3 miles (11.6 km). The land beyond the pipe line and to the left of the road is a wildlife refuge. Hunting is prohibited within the refuge. The climbing now becomes serious, and you next pass an old road to the right. Near the top you bear right on a firebreak where you are really out in the sun. The route continues upward, but gently, passing a gas well at 8.6 miles (13.8 km). At 9.1 miles (14.5 km) you turn right on the Laurel Highland Trail at the junction with another management road. You pass milepost 60 at 9.9 miles (15.8 km), and soon you cross the grassy road where you turned some three of four hours ago. From here on, retrace your steps to your car.

Allegheny
National Forest

17

Hearts Content Scenic Area

Distance: 1.1 miles (1.8 km)
Time: ¾ hour
Rise: 110 feet (35 m)
Highlights: Virgin timber, log display
Maps: USGS 7½' Cherry Grove, Cobham

White pine was the most valuable tree growing in Penn's Woods during the nineteenth century logging era. But white pine doesn't belong to the region's climax vegetation. It is, instead, an opportunistic tree that grows in large stands following some disaster to the mature forest, such as a wind storm or fire. The great stands of white pine that the nineteenth century loggers exploited in Pennsylvania are attributed to the fires of 1644. By then, there were people settled along the Atlantic Coast. They wrote home all summer about the poor air quality, as the smoke from many forest fires rolled out of the interior.

This white pine made Pennsylvania first in timber production after the Civil War. Production continued to rise until late in the nineteenth century. But, by then, several western states had passed Pennsylvania in output of timber.

At Hearts Content a small tract of white pine has been preserved much as the loggers found it. Unlike many other small tracts of virgin timber in Pennsylvania the circumstances are well

Virgin Timber

known. In 1922 the firm of Wheeler and Dusenbury donated 20 acres to the government. In 1931 another 100 acres were purchased by the federal government, bringing the Hearts Content Scenic Area to its present size.

The trailhead for this hike is the Hearts Content picnic area, and the directions for reaching it are the same as for Hickory Creek (hike 29). The Tom Run Hike (hike 19) also leaves from the same parking area but now you want the obvious trail that leads to the virgin timber and log display.

You come immediately to a marker that proclaims Hearts Content a registered Natural Landmark. The trail is marked only with very occasional yellow arrows, and soon one directs you to bear right past a dead pine. Many of the white pines are dead or dying. In the parlance of foresters, the stand is "over mature", and we are watching the pines being replaced by shade-tolerant hemlocks. Already many of these hemlocks are very large trees in their own right. If left to itself, this forest would reach its "climax," or "steady-state population"—probably a pure stand of sugar maples.

At 0.4 mile (0.6 km) you reach a

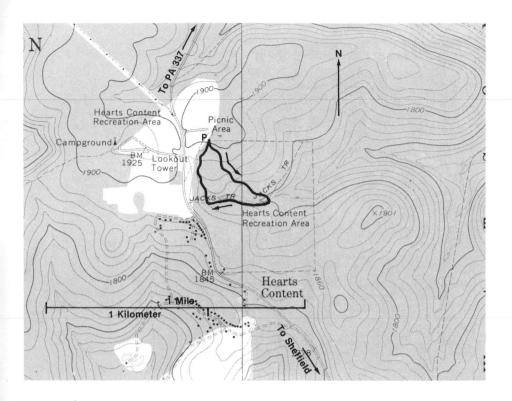

memorial to the Wheelers and Dusen-
burys, who ran their logging business
for over a century. Immediately behind
the memorial are several springs that
constitute the source of the West
Branch of Tionesta Creek. All about you
are the large white pines. Many companies cut pines this size and sawed
them into standard-size timbers and
boards. Wheeler and Dusenbury
specialized in long timbers. Their mill at
Endeavor could cut logs up to 100 feet
long. These long logs were primarily
used as bridge timbers, but earlier in
the century they had been used for
masts and spars on sailing ships.

Such logs could not be loaded on a
single log car. Unless two steam-
powered log loaders were available,
they had to be loaded by hand. Wheeler
and Dusenbury were still supplying such
special timbers when most of the rest
of Penn's Woods had been cut over.

Beyond the memorial, you cross the
headwaters of the West Branch and
head back upstream. Other trees growing here are red maple, yellow birch,
black birch, black cherry and white ash.
At 0.8 mile (1.3 km) you turn right
again, and at 1.1 miles (1.7 km) you
reach a shelter housing a white pine
timber squared by hand. Before
railroads and steam-powered sawmills
were built in all corners of the state, the
only way to get timber to market was to
raft it down the rivers leading to the
Allegheny and Ohio. In those days,
timbers were squared by hand and then
rafted as far as Cincinnati, Ohio, and
Louisville, Kentucky.

After leaving the log exhibit, bear right along the edge of the woods, and you will shortly be back at the parking lot.

For another view of the scenic area, cross the road and climb Wheeler Tower. From there you can see how the ancient white pines tower over their neighbors.

18

Cornplanter State Forest

Distance: 3.6 miles (5.9 km)
Time: 2 hours
Rise: 520 feet (160 m)
Highlights: Oil wells, old and new; forestry
   demonstration area
Maps: USGS 7½' West Hickory; Cornplanter
   State Forest Public Use map

With a total area of only 1,200 acres, Cornplanter appears to be the smallest state forest save for Valley Forge, which is only 10 acres around a fire tower. Cornplanter is located on the border of Allegheny National Forest, just west of the Allegheny River between Pleasantville and Tionesta. The forest is named for Chief Cornplanter (1750-1836) of the Seneca Indians. Chief Cornplanter is credited with keeping peace between the newly independent and vulnerable United States of America and the League of the Iroquois.

Most of Pennsylvania's forest lands consist of small parcels owned by a great many private owners. One task of state foresters is to advise landowners how to manage their lands for timber and pulpwood production. To this end, as well as for environmental education, the Hunter Run Demonstration Area and Lashure Trails were developed. Cornplanter also has a cross-country ski trail. This hike samples all these attractions. Despite an occasional wet spot, ordinary walking shoes should be fine.

The trailhead is reached from PA 36 at a point 2.2 miles from the junction with US 62 at the west end of the

bridge over the Allegheny and 7.2 miles from the junction with PA 27 in Pleasantville. Turn north at a sign for Neilltown on the Hunter Run Road (LR 27005), go 1.0 mile and then turn left at the sign for the Hunter Run Demonstration Area. Follow the narrow road for 0.2 mile to the parking area at the information board and registration box. Pick up a brochure so you can interpret the numbered posts on the nature trail you'll soon reach.

To start the hike, walk back down this same road. On the right, you pass blocks of trees planted in an old field as part of the forestry demonstration. Next to the road, black cherry, white ash and larch have been planted. Only the larch are in evidence, and the hardwoods may have been browsed by deer. Farther back are plantings of red oak, sugar maple, tulip poplar, two kinds of fir, five kinds of spruce and six kinds of pine. At the small pond, built to provide water for forest fire trucks, turn left on LaShure Trail No. 1. Ray LaShure was a forest fire warden who led one of the

Modern Oil Well

first fire fighting crews in the area. Old apple trees survive from when these fields were part of a farm. Soon the trail enters the woods, and you find it liberally provided with benches. The blue blazes used to mark Trail No. 1 are finally encountered at 0.4 miles (0.6 km). If the blazes look a little misshapen, it's because they are supposed to look like footprints. LaShure Trail No. 1 is set up as a nature trail. At 0.5 mile (0.8 km) you turn left on

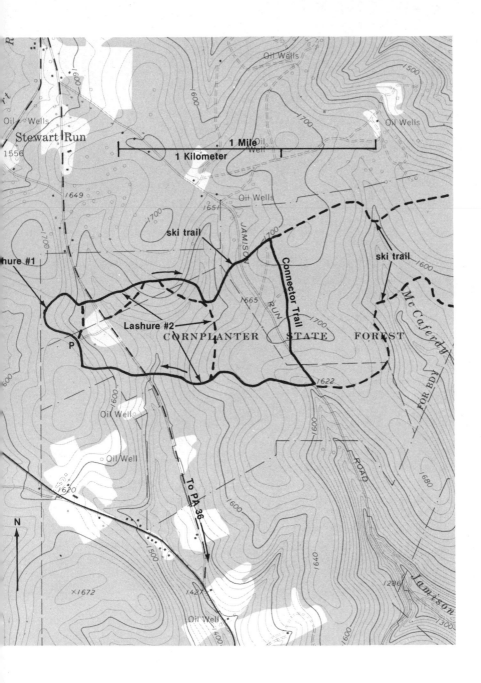

orange-blazed LaShure Trail No. 2. Soon you cross the Hunter Run Road, and just beyond you cross two branches of Hunter Run on log bridges.

Turn left on the blue-blazed old road at 0.8 mile (1.3 km). These blue blazes are rectangular, as this is the Hunter Run Ski Trail. The orange-blazed LaShure Trail soon turns right, but you continue ahead, ignoring an unblazed old road to the left.

An old oil well is reached at 1.1 miles (1.7 km), and shortly you come to the first of many active wells. Drake's Well, the first oil well ever drilled, is only ten miles west of here, along the banks of Oil Creek. The yield from most wells is low, comparable to that from Drake's Well. The pumps may run for only a few minutes each week. The rest of the time, oil slowly collects in the well. Most of the oil wells brought into production since 1973 have been in or around old oil fields such as this. Pennsylvania crude oil commands a premium price for its value in making lubricants.

Next you turn right and then cross another branch of Hunter Run on a log bridge, briefly rejoining the orange-blazed LaShure Trail, which uses the same bridge. At 1.3 miles (2.1 km) you pass through a clearing for another old oil well, and soon you bear right on a jeep road. Then you turn left at a junction of jeep roads. The blazing at this turn is obscure when the leaves are out. At 1.6 miles (2.5 km) cross the un-paved Jamison Run Road. Continue into the woods on the far side and then turn right past the ruins of what was apparently another oil well. At 1.9 miles (3.1 km) you turn right on the red-blazed Connector Trail, which is an old woods road that passes some more oil wells. A jeep road to an active well is crossed at 2.1 miles (3.4 km), and soon the red blazes bear left off the old woods road. The trail beyond here has not been cleared for hikers. The brush must be under the snow when the trail is used by skiers. Continue along the unblazed old road and then bear left on the Jamison Run Road. At 2.6 miles (4.1 km) turn right on the blue-blazed ski trail, just across from a gated road. Soon you bear right off this old road, and then bear right again onto another woods road.

Next you turn left onto another woods road, and at 3.1 miles (5.0 km) you turn right onto trail. Turn left on the orange-blazed LaShure Trail at 3.3 miles (5.3 km) and then cross a log bridge over a stream. A small clearing to the left of the trail is a woodcock management area. A woodcock is a small game bird with a long beak and short legs. Other animals also benefit from the varied habitat. At 3.4 miles (5.5 km) you cross Hunter Run on a log bridge. The blue blazes then turn right, but you follow the orange blazes across the Hunter Run Road. Beyond the road, you enter an evergreen plantation, and soon you are back at your car.

19

Tom Run

Distance: 4.0 miles (6.4 km)
Time: 2¼ hours
Rise: 400 feet (120 m)
Highlight: Virgin timber
Maps: USGS 7½' Cherry Grove, Cobham

Within Allegheny National Forest the Tanbark Trail, which once stretched from Tionesta Scenic Area to US 62, used to be second in length only to the North Country Trail. The original or southern route of the North Country Trail crossed some private land within Allegheny National Forest. When the owners began to have second thoughts about the North Country Trail, the Forest Service simply abandoned the original route. The North Country Trail was relocated onto the Tanbark Trail, reducing the Tanbark Trail to a nine-mile section from near Dunham Siding to US 62. Nevertheless, the Tanbark passes through or near some of the most beautiful parts of Allegheny National Forest.

This hike uses part of the Tanbark Trail near Hearts Content Scenic Area and an unmarked old railroad grade of Wheeler and Dusenbury to make a loop through the valley of Tom Run and the uppermost part of the West Branch of Tionesta Creek. Since much of the path is not clear but goes through deep ferns and grass, hiking boots are in order.

The trailhead is the picnic area at Hearts Content Scenic Area, the same as for Hickory Creek Trail (Hike 29). No need to park in the lot for Hickory Creek Trail. If space permits, you can use the picnic area lot, which has some shade around the edges. Avoid the obvious trail that leads to the virgin timber and log display. Instead follow the trail to the left that seems to lead only to the men's outhouse. This trail is not marked but is fairly easy to follow as it parallels the northern boundary of the Hearts Content Scenic Area. Then it swings to the right, and at 0.3 mile (0.5 km) you pass a sign case and boundary marker and cross a corner of the scenic area. Immediately you are among the giant white pines. Note the size of one giant that has fallen across the trail. Listen, if you can, to the sound of wind in the pine tops far above you. This trail is not maintained, so care is required in following it. Bear left at a fork in the trail, and soon you pass another sign case. At 0.5 mile (0.8 km) you turn left on the Tanbark Trail. The Tanbark is marked with blue "eye" blazes. Follow the Tanbark over a low ridge and down the north slope. At the bottom of the hill, 1.1 miles (1.8 km), turn right on an old railroad grade, which immediately enters a meadow. The old railroad is difficult to follow across the meadow,

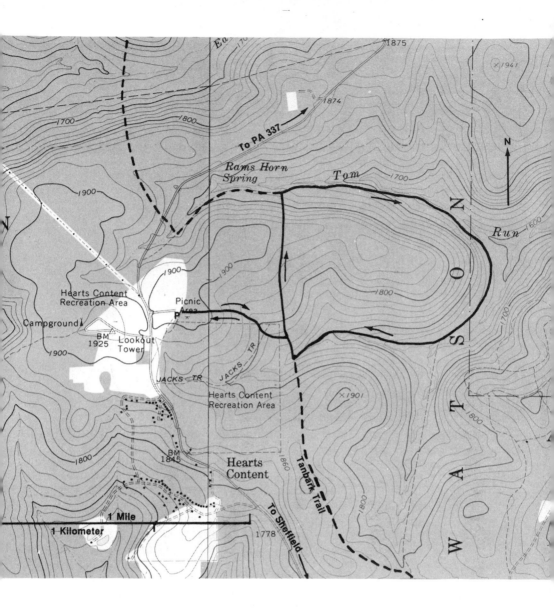

since you have to zig and zag to avoid wet spots. But make sure you pick it up again on the far side. The grade is much easier to follow when it tunnels through the hemlocks than when it crosses the open meadows.

At one point in a meadow, a family of grouse flushed, the chicks heading off in one direction, the hen in the other. The hen circled back, displaying her "broken wing" and cheeping piteously. She was trying to draw me away from her chicks. Soon the wing healed miraculously, and she circled around me to collect her brood.

At 1.9 miles (3.0 km) are a pair of

White Pine

crossings of Tom Run. If the water level makes the crossings difficult, you can avoid them by bearing right at the first one. At 2.1 miles (3.3 km) you pass a marker nailed to a tree, which indicates you are crossing into State Game Land 29. A trail diverges to the left at 2.3 miles (3.6 km), but you stick to the old railroad grade and begin the gentle climb back to the plateau. The clover-like flower growing here is oxalis. At 2.7 miles (4.3 km) you catch your first sight of the West Branch and confirm that you are indeed now walking upstream. At some point here you leave the state game land. At 2.9 miles (4.6 km) keep right where a siding diverges to the left, and at 3.1 miles (5.0 km) you bear left off the railroad grade and cross a small side stream. On the other side, you

regain the railroad grade and continue. The railroad bridge is long gone, although elsewhere in this valley traces of old bridges remain. Soon a siding comes in from the right, and at 3.4 miles (5.4 km) you turn right on the Tanbark Trail. There is a pole bridge crossing the stream at this point. This stream, coming from Hearts Content, is the major source of the West Branch of Tionesta Creek. Turn left on the unmarked trail to Hearts Content Picnic Area at 3.5 miles (5.6 km), and retrace your steps to the parking lot.

Additional hiking opportunities at Hearts Content are Hickory Creek Trail (Hike 29), Hearts Content Scenic Area (Hike 17) and Slater Run, which also uses the Tanbark Trail (Hike 21).

20

Clear Creek State Park

Distance: 5.2 miles (8.3 km)
Time: 3¼ hours
Rise: 880 feet (270 meters)
Highlights: Evergreen plantations, pileated
   woodpeckers
Maps: USGS 7½' Sigel; state park trail map

Clear Creek is a small state park just across the Clarion River from Allegheny National Forest. There are about 15 miles of trails in this park of only 1,200 acres. The park occupies the valley of Clear Creek between PA 949 and the Clarion. Many of the 17 trails used to cross Clear Creek on footbridges, but heavy rains on 9 June 1981 took out most of these bridges. This hike is designed to make use of the bridges that survive. You'll traverse the camping area in the park, so observe the prohibition on pets in that area. Despite some rocks and a few wet areas, good walking shoes should be adequate.

Clear Creek State Park is on PA 949, and the trailhead at the Beach House parking area is 3.9 miles from the junction with PA 36 in Sigel, which in turn is about 7 miles north of exit 13 on I-80 in Brookville. The hike starts on the Clear Creek Trail which you will find in the far left hand corner of the parking lot to the left of the water pump. This trail, like all those in the park, is marked with white, diamond-shaped blazes. Double blazes are used to mark turns and triple blazes to mark intersections and ends of trails.

You bear left almost immediately at a side trail that leads to the beach. Continue through a Norway spruce plantation with occasional aspen volunteers. Witch-hazel is also found along the trail, and at one place you pass a service berry that has grown to the size of a small tree. Soon you cross the Phyllis Run Trail, and shortly after that, the Ridge Trail diverges to the left. The trail then passes through a rhododendron thicket. Note the association between this shrub and the many spring seeps. Next, you pass the Big Coon Trail and the Little Coon Trail, both of which descend towards Clear Creek. Black cherry is found along this section of the trail, and at another spot you see a large sandstone boulder on its leisurely way to the creek below.

At 0.8 mile (1.3 km) you arrive at the top of a steep bank above the creek, adorned with a white pine tree, and soon you turn left on an old railroad grade. This may be the old Frazier Railroad that served two steam-powered sawmills further up the Clear Creek valley in the 1860's. It is not known whether the Frazier Railroad even had a locomotive; it could have used horses. There was no connecting railroad along the Clarion at that time, so the lumber must have been floated downstream on rafts or flatboats.

Immediately beyond, you cross the pipeline swath that cuts across the valley. Then you pass a walk-in picnic area, and at 0.9 mile (1.5 km) you cross Sawmill Run and continue on the old tram road.

The Sawmill Trail comes in from the left at 1.1 miles (1.7 km). A bit beyond, a piped spring comes out from underneath the trail.

One of the largest birds you may see in these woods is the pileated woodpecker. This crow-sized bird is the largest woodpecker in the world next to the extraordinarily rare ivory-billed woodpecker. Its presence is usually revealed by oval holes chiseled up to eight inches deep into trees. Its flight is swooping and reveals large white under-wing patches. The call is like that of a flicker but louder, deeper, and woodier.

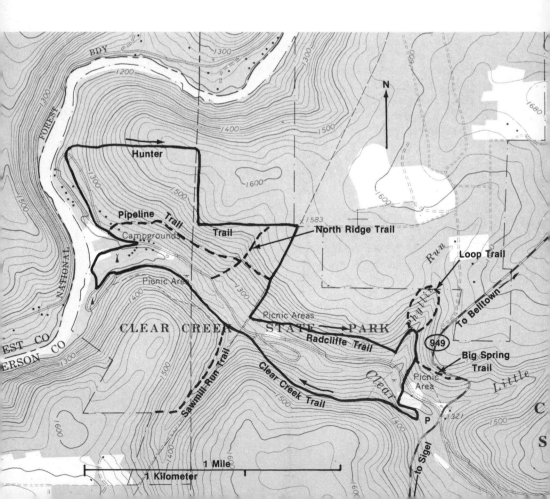

Clear Creek Trail

The holes it makes in search of ants and grubs do not kill the tree, and its radical surgery may actually save the tree from these parasites.

At 1.3 miles (2.0 km) keep left at a junction with the Oxshoe Trail which diverges to the right, and at 1.5 miles (2.4 km) you bear right on the gravel road in the campground. In traversing the campground you pass drinking water and cross Clear Creek on the road bridge. The Clarion River is on your left, and some benches are provided for enjoying the view. At 1.8 miles (2.9 km) turn left on a paved road. Soon the Pipeline Trail, which can be used to shorten this hike, diverges to the right. Keep right where the road splits. You can avoid some of this road walking by using the jogging trail to your left—at some risk of being run over by a speeding jogger.

Bear right to the River Trail at 2.3 miles (3.6 km), cross the paved road, and shortly turn right on the Hunter Trail. You now begin the only real climb on this hike.

The Hunter Trail is marked both with the standard white diamond blazes and with large irregular shaped white blazes. The latter show that this trail separates the part of the park open to hunting on your left from the part closed to hunting on your right. The top of the hill is reached at 2.7 miles (4.3 km), and shortly the trail turns right. It continues in this new direction until it reaches the edge of Clear Creek Valley. After starting to descend, it turns sharply left, regains the hilltop, and continues past a junction with the North Ridge Trail at 3.6 miles (5.7 km). Turn right on the pipeline and note the larch trees planted here to soften the visual impact of the swath.

A large boulder at 3.8 miles (6.0 km) provides a view across the valley. The swath is a good place to see deer. Soon the Pipeline Trail joins from the right, and you turn left on the Radcliffe Trail at 3.9 miles (6.3 km). The Radcliffe Trail proceeds through a plantation of white pine and Norway spruce. Where the trail meets some red pines, it jogs farther up the hillside. At 4.6 miles (7.4 km) turn left on the Phyllis Run Trail in the midst of another spruce plantation. You get several good views of Phyllis Run as you pass an unsafe piped spring. Bypass the longer loop, cross Phyllis Run, and head back down the other side. Shortly the Big Spring Trail diverges left, and at 4.9 miles (7.9 km) you turn left on the paved park road. Keep right, and in only 50 yards you find a flight of steps leading down to several picnic shelters. Cut through the picnic area to the dam and use the foot bridge to cross. A plaque says the dam was built by the Civilian Conservation Corps in 1934.

Beyond the dam turn left and pass between the beach and beach house to the gated access road. You are back at the beach house parking lot and your car.

This hike uses only four of the seventeen trails in Clear Creek State Park. There is plenty of additional hiking.

21

Slater Run

Distance: 5.5 miles (8.7 km)
Time: 3 hours
Rise: 650 feet (200 meters)
Highlights: Tanbark Trail, mountain streams
Maps: USGS 7½' Cobham, Youngville; Hiker's
　Guide to Allegheny National Forest,
　map no. 12

This hike uses the northernmost portion of the Tanbark Trail and an old railroad grade to take you on a delightful circuit hike in the Allegheny Front area. The tanbark referred to is that of the eastern hemlock, *Tsuga canadensis*. In the nineteenth century, tannic acid was extracted from hemlock bark and used to tan hides. It was cheaper to bring the hides to the bark than the bark to the hides, so Penn's Woods was filled with tanneries, large and small. The leather companies bought large tracts of hemlocks to assure themselves a supply of bark. On occasion, hemlocks were cut solely for their bark and the logs left to rot in the woods.

About the turn of the century, 65 of the 120 largest tanneries formed the United States Leather Company. U.S. Leather then formed Central Pennsylvania Lumber Company to cut its hemlock forests. But time was running out for the tanneries. Most of the hemlocks were soon gone, and the tanneries began to close. Many of the towns they had spawned became ghost towns. Much of the leather was used

for harnesses for horses, mules and oxen. With the coming of the internal combustion engine, the harness market collapsed. Leather was also used for belts to run machines in factories, but the electric motor largely eliminated this application. Synthetic tannic acid was developed, too, ending the need for natural supplies. So the Tanbark Trail reminds us of the rise and fall of the tanning industry in Penn's Woods.

The Allegheny Front Area is one of the four largest roadless areas in Allegheny National Forest. It is bordered by US 62 on the west and PA 337 on the east. It includes most or all of the valleys of Slater and South Slater runs, Boarding House Run, Clark Run, Hedgehog Run and Charley Run. Oil and gas drilling precludes Allegheny Front from designation as a wilderness area.

The trailhead is located on US 62, 8.9 miles north of the PA 337 junction in Tidioute and 6.7 miles south of US 6. There is ample parking on the river side of the highway, both north and south of the Tanbark trailhead. Hiking boots are

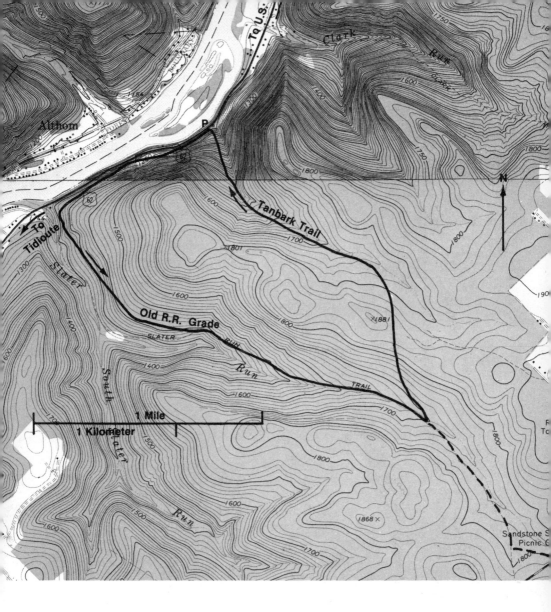

in order, owing to many wet areas and a steep scramble up the side of a road cut on US 62.

To start the hike, head south along US 62. Keep to the left side, facing the heavy traffic. This part isn't much fun, so hurry along. Pass a cabin and some posted private land. You are looking for the old railroad grade up the hillside, but it can't be seen from the highway.

Avoid a couple of old roads on private land. They aren't railroads. The public land is at the steepest part of the hillside. The old railroad grade is 0.6 mile (0.9 km) from the Tanbark trailhead, and your landmarks are a small concrete wall followed immediately by a small sign facing the other way which says 6/50. The sign is a state transportation department distance marker. Here you scramble up the steep bank above the sign. A few yards north, the railroad grade has been destroyed by the highway. A few yards south it is even higher above the road. Once you gain the old railroad grade, turn right and climb higher still. A footway is discernible along the outside of the old railroad. Early logging railroads were innocent of surveying. They were usually narrow gauge and so poorly built that one can have great difficulty following them today. This railroad appears to be a late model. It is standard gauge, and the even gradient indicates good surveying.

The trail makes a cool dark tunnel under the large hemlocks. At 0.8 mile (1.2 km) bear left at a fork in the railroad grade. You immediately cross under a pole line and can see a house to the right. The railroad continues through hemlock groves. You can hear Slater Run below, but you won't see it for some time yet. At 1.3 miles (2.1 km) keep left where a faint trail diverges to the right. The hillside becomes rockier with conglomerate and sandstone boulders, some of them quite large. Another trail converges from the right at 1.9 miles (3.1 km). Here a boulder has slid partway across the grade, evidence that these rocks do move on occasion.

Soon you come to a side stream with considerable flow, one of many wet places. Next you reach the edge of the mountain laurel belt. I suspect the laurel is associated with a certain layer of

bedrock. At 2.4 miles (3.9 km) Slater Run is close at hand, and a faint trail leads over to this appealing mountain stream. The railroad grade has become poorly defined. However, it doesn't make any wild turns, so continue ahead. Soon the mountain laurel closes in to define the trail. A bullet-riddled pipe sticking out of the ground at 2.7 miles (4.3 km) is the only sign of oil drilling on this hike. Soon you cross Slater Run and continue to climb very gently, leaving the mountain laurel behind.

The junction with the blue-"eye"-blazed Tanbark Trail is reached at 3.1 miles (5.0 km). Turn left and cross Slater Run on a bridge. Then climb past a campsite at the top of the bank and continue climbing to the broad ridge top. At 3.8 miles (6.1 km) turn left on an old road. After a bit, you notice that you are now descending slowly. Next you can see Boarding House Run to your right among some fair-sized hemlocks. The Tanbark Trail is now definitely descending. After crossing a side stream, you bear right off the old road at 5.3 miles (8.4 km) and descend steeply among large black cherry and hemlock trees. As you cross the pole line swath, you get a good view of Boarding House Run. A few more steps and you are back at the highway.

This hike could be extended by following the Tanbark out to the Sandstone Springs picnic area on PA 337 before taking it down Boarding House Run.

State Game Lands 74

In-and-out distance: 5.8 miles (9.8 km)
Time: 3 hours
Rise: 100 feet (30 m)
Highlight: Baker Trail
Maps: USGS 7½' Corsica; Baker Trail Guide
    Book map #14; Sportsmen's Recreation
    Map—State Game Lands 74

One of the nicest sections of the Baker Trail runs south of Cook Forest, crossing State Game Lands No. 74 along Mill Creek. (This is a different Mill Creek than the one in Allegheny National Forest.)

In the early nineteenth century, when water was the only dependable source of power, nearly every stream had one or more grist mills or sawmills. Eventually, coal replaced water as a source of energy. Much of the coal in western Pennsylvania is a high-sulfur variety. Air and water work together to convert this sulfur into sulfuric acid, causing acid mine drainage from old mines which is

quite harmful to nearby waterways. Currently the only way to prevent this acid mine drainage is to strip mine the coal seam in question, which destroys the old mine tunnels. Since many old mines are very shallow, much acid mine drainage could be eliminated, provided the strip mining is done in accordance with Pennsylvania law.

While the lower part of Mill Creek, which you cross on the way to the trailhead, shows evidence of acid mine drainage, the upper part of Mill Creek in Game Lands 74 appears to be free of it. There is even some life in the stream.

Game Lands 74 is located north of I-80 and east of Clarion. The trailhead is a bit complicated to reach, so pay careful attention. From exit 11 on I-80, take US 322 west for about 4 miles to Strattanville. Turn right on Perry Street and follow it northeast for 6.7 miles to the crossroads of Fisher, crossing Mill Creek and the game lands along the way. Turn right at the church and go south for 1.2 miles. Here you bear left and follow the road down into Mill Creek

Valley for 1.4 miles to a parking area, just before a bridge over the creek. You may park on either side of the road, but there is more shade on the left. Several ways to shortcut this approach to the trailhead can be found with the help of the game commission map and dry roads. You could also arrange a car shuttle.

Ordinary walking shoes should be fine for this hike. If you want to wear your hiking boots, they will help you cross Updike Run.

To start the hike, step over or around the gate on the emergency road near the creek. Make sure you are headed upstream on Mill Creek, not Pendleton Run, which you must cross immediately on stepping stones. Pendleton Run supports a growth of hemlocks and rhododendrons. Just beyond, you join the yellow-blazed Baker Trail and continue upstream along Mill Creek on the game commission management road. Trees along the trail are black cherry, white oak, red maple, occasional white pines, and many hemlocks, large and

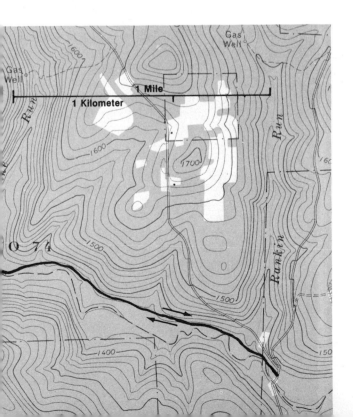

Deer Tracks

small. Don't be alarmed if you see blazes at right angles to the trail. They do not indicate a turn but are only a curious variation of blazing on the Baker Trail. Occasionally, unmarked fishermen's trails do lead off to the creek. At 1.4 miles (2.2 km) the creek comes back to your side of the valley, and soon you reach a large game food plot. There is also some aspen around the borders of this meadow but no evidence of beaver. The game commission road ends here at the food plot, but continue across the plot in a straight line. At the far side, you cross Updike Run and pick up the trail again on an old woods road.

The trail jogs left at 2.0 miles (3.2 km) and climbs a bank. Here you enter a dark enchanted forest of hemlocks. Continue through the hemlocks to 2.9 miles (4.7 km) where you meet a road.

This is just beyond the game lands boundary and marks the turn-around point. The Baker Trail guide indicates that the Baker Trail continues on private land north of Mill Creek, but my search in this direction found no blazes or footway. The only blaze I could find was one that was peeling on the bridge abutment. Perhaps the Baker Trail takes up road walking at this point. Retrace your steps to your car.

Also in Game Lands 74 you could follow the Baker Trail up Pendleton Run or follow the management road downstream from the parking area. At one time the North Country Trail was to follow Baker to this point and then head downstream along Mill Run. It appears now that it will follow the Clarion River on lands recently acquired by the Western Pennsylvania Conservancy.

Cook Forest State Park

Distance: 6.3 miles (10.2 km)
Time: 4 hours
Rise: 1,220 feet (370 meters)
Highlights: Virgin timber, lookout tower
Maps: USGS 7½' Cooksburg; state park map;
    Baker Trail maps

Logging started early in what is now Cook Forest State Park. John Cook began cutting along Toms Run in 1828. Rafts made of squared white pine logs were floated to Pittsburgh. This business was continued by Cook's son, Anthony, and then in turn by the grandchildren. A small patch of timber, only a short distance from the sawmill on Toms Run, had been left standing with the intention that it be cut just before the sawmill was dismantled. In the 1920's the Cook Forest Association raised $200,000, and with $450,000 from the state, used it to purchase Cook Forest State Park. Thus one of the largest stands of virgin white pine remaining in Pennsylvania was saved from the axe. At other locations in the park, virgin hemlock is found. But what man has saved, nature may still ravage. Violent wind storms, one in 1956 and another in 1976, devastated different parts of the forest, felling windrows of trees. The park has also been damaged by floods. In June 1981 one flood washed out several footbridges across Toms Run, severing the Baker and other trails. This hike visits several areas of virgin timber, Cook Forest fire tower and a lookout over the Clarion River, using parts of the Baker Trail not destroyed in the storms of 1976 and 1981.

Cook Forest State Park is on PA 36 about 15 miles north of exit 13 on I-80 at Brookville. The hike starts from the entrance to the Ridge Campground on PA 36 at the top of the hill above the bridge over the Clarion. There is a parking lot between the highway and the campground. There are a number of wet areas on this hike, but the footway is good, and you should be able to do the hike with ordinary walking shoes.

To start the hike, cross PA 36 and bear right on the exit from the one-way road to the fire tower. Where the exit road splits, keep right on the part which heads you back to the highway. At the point where you return to PA 36, find the Mohawk Trail and turn left. Immediately you are in a beautiful stand of virgin hemlocks interspersed with a few white pines and giant beeches. At 0.8 mile (1.3 km) turn right on the Tower Road. At the top of a rise look carefully for the unsigned River Trail crossing

and turn right on this trail at 1.2 miles (1.9 km). The River Trail descends to the Clarion, and about halfway down there is a confusing stretch where the trail splits into several paths. The trail you want crosses the bottom of the draw and continues down the far side. There are several large stands of rhododendron along this part of the River Trail as well as a patch of mountain laurel. The laurel usually blooms in mid-June and the rhododendron in early July.

At the bottom of the hill the Baker Trail comes in from the right past a natural gas well. You see one token yellow blaze at this point. The Baker Trail is not blazed through the park. Instead it is marked with signs at trail junctions and road crossings. Take a good look at the Clarion, down which you can see Hemlock Island, and then turn left (upstream), still on the River Trail. There is more rhododendron along the river. At 2.0 miles (3.2 km) you cross a meadow and then a side stream. The trail starts to draw away from the river and reclimb the hill. The climb is gentle until you reach 2.3 miles (3.7 km), where the trail turns sharply left and climbs steeply for the next 400 yards to the base of Cook Forest lookout tower. The best views from the top are north up Toms Run and east up the Clarion.

Back on the ground, follow the heavily-used trail to the Seneca Trail junction and turn left to Seneca Point. Seneca Point is a natural vista down the Clarion River. Then backtrack on the Seneca Trail and continue past the restrooms and parking area along the edge of the hill. At 3.3 miles (5.2 km) the Deer Park Trail diverges to the left and you start down the side of the hill through another stand of virgin hemlock and white pine. Soon you enter the area damaged by the tornado of 11 July

1976. The trail has been reestablished so it is still easy to follow, and there is a view of the Clarion below. Soon you reenter the woods where the trail has been dug into the steep hillside, and at 3.7 miles (5.9 km) you are at the bottom of the hill.

At 3.8 miles (6.0 km) you cross PA 36 with care and continue on the River Road to the park office. (The office parking lot makes an alternative trailhead.) There is a display of old photos of Cook Forest, and you can check at the office whether the swing bridge across Toms Run has been replaced. If it has, you should use the Birch Trail, to avoid walking through the Indian cabin area. If the swing bridge is still out, move upstream behind the office and turn right across the bridge to the cabin area. (Birch Trail is just around the bend, next to PA 36.) Pass the Indian Trail which diverges right just beyond the bridge and continue through the cabin area. Go between cabin nos. 5 and 6 and pick up the unsigned Rhododendron Trail, which proceeds upstream along Toms Run.

At 4.1 miles (6.6 km) you pass the site of the swing bridge across Toms Run. You will cross Toms Run here if the bridge has been rebuilt. The Rhododendron Trail swings away from the run and gradually climbs the east side of the valley passing a natural gas well along the way. At 4.7 miles (7.5 km) turn left on the Joyce Kilmer Trail and then shortly left again on the Indian Trail and very shortly right on the Longfellow and Baker trails.

This is the heart of the forest cathedral. The 200 foot white pines you find here are truly awesome. An ordinary white pine would top off where the first branches on these monarchs begin. Were all Penns Wood's like this from the lake to the sea only 200 years ago? Considering all the demands on

Clarion River

forests today—not only timber and pulp but firewood, biomass and even a new resource base for the chemical industry—can any forest on this planet ever be left long enough to grow trees like these again?

Continue down the Longfellow Trail and wander up and down the lettered side trails as the spirit moves you. At 5.3 miles (8.5 km) on the Longfellow Trail you pass the memorial fountain (now dry) and shortly emerge on the paved road next to the Log Cabin Inn. Turn left on the road facing traffic and cross the stone bridge over Toms Run. Pass the Liggett-Baker Trail and continue to the Ridge Trail where you cross the road and start the climb back to the campground. The climb passes through more large hemlocks, reaching the top of the hill at 5.9 miles (9.5 km). At the end of the Ridge Trail in the campground turn left on the paved road and follow it to the entrance parking lot and your car.

This hike has used only six of the 27 miles of hiking trails in Cook Forest State Park, so there are many additional hiking opportunities. The Sawmill Nature Trail, just beyond the Log Cabin Inn, is one. Another is the Baker Trail, which leads into the more remote regions of the park along Browns Run and to a 170-acre stand of virgin hemlock near Greenwood Road.

Hemlock Run

Distance: 6.8 miles (11.0 km)
Time: 4 hours
Rise: 300 feet (90 m)
Highlight: North Country Trail
Maps: USGS 7½' Cornplanter Bridge, Westline;
  Hiker's Guide to Allegheny National Forest,
  maps 2 and 3

The National Trails System Act of 1968 designated the Pacific Crest Trail and the Appalachian Trail as National Scenic Trails. The act named fourteen other trails for study and possible addition to the system. One of these was the North Country Trail, from Crown Point in New York to the Missouri River in North Dakota. If completed, the North Country Trail will extend about 3,200 miles, the longest in the world. In 1980, Congress designated the North Country Trail as a National Scenic Trail but said it must be built by volunteers. Meanwhile, a section of the North Country Trail, 100 miles long, had already been built across Allegheny National Forest, from the New York state line to Pennsylvania State Game Land 24, where it joins the Baker Trail. Much of the North Country Trail in Allegheny National Forest was built by the Allegheny Outdoor Club. The Baker Trail was built by the Pittsburgh Council of the American Youth Hostels.

This hike follows an exceptionally appealing section of the North Country Trail along Hemlock Run, between PA 59 and PA 321 at Chappel Fork. It is

organized as a car shuttle hike, and it is almost entirely downhill. The car shuttle is simple, involving only the two highways already mentioned. Leave one car at the end of the hike on PA 321. Caution! The North Country Trail crosses PA 321 at two different places. The crossing you want is the more northern one. It is 5.5 miles north of the junction with PA 59 at the Bradford Ranger Station. The crossing is signed, and there is parking for several cars on the west side of the road. Then drive your other car north 4.5 miles and turn left on PA 59 for 2.3 miles. The North Country Trail crossing of PA 59 is also signed, and there is parking for a couple of cars on Forest Road 265, just off the highway. The many stream crossings make this a low-water hike, and you should wear hiking boots.

To start the hike, continue along Forest Road 265. There are no blazes along this section. At 0.1 mile (0.2 km) the forest road is gated off, and you turn right on an old road. Here you pick up the white "eye" blazes. There is no sign at this turn. At 0.4 mile (0.6 km) you bear right off the old road, but at

To Warren

N

North Country Trail

1 mile
1 Kilometer

To PA 321

To PA 59

321

To Kane

0.5 mile (0.8 km) you bear right again on what appears to be the same road. A structure, apparently abandoned, is visible through the trees to the left. A variation of the "eye" blaze is used along this section to mark turns. The small rectangle is placed on the side of the large rectangle to indicate the direction of the turn. This is effective, but it does take a large tree to carry the blaze. At 0.6 mile (1.0 km) you continue straight ahead where another road diverges to the left, and soon you cross a small meadow. You jog left across Forest Road 517 at 1.3 miles (2.1 km), passing a large service berry. The small stream to your left is Hemlock Run, and you will follow it as it cuts its way down to Chappel Bay. Smaller streams enter from each side, and Hemlock Run grows with each addition. Hemlock Run makes a deeper cut into the plateau

where you come to some large sandstone and conglomerate boulders, on their slow slide into the stream.

At 2.1 miles (3.4 km) you dodge across the corner of a clearing past House Rock. When viewed through the trees the slanting sides of House Rock look like the roof of a cabin. The first crossing of Hemlock Run is at 2.3 miles (3.7 km), but the next isn't until 2.7 miles (4.3 km). Then three come in rapid succession. At the last of these note the large hemlocks. Farther along you pick up an old railroad grade, and the valley begins to widen out. At 3.7 miles (5.9 km) there are two more crossings of Hemlock Run, and at 4.3 miles (6.8 km) there are another two crossings. Occasionally, the trail climbs the bank to avoid a crossing. The railroad must have transported logs to the Central Pennsylvania Lumber Com-

Bridge over Chappel Fork

pany mill at Kinzua. This town is now submerged beneath Allegheny Reservoir.

Turn left at 4.8 miles (7.6 km). Ahead, you can see the waters of Chappel Bay. The railroad continues beneath them, on its way to Kinzua. As you continue along the hillside, you soon pick up an old road. At 5.4 miles (8.6 km) you jog right across a pipe-line swath. Below you, Chappel Fork is already a free flowing stream again. Next you turn left on another Central Pennsylvania Lumber railroad grade and follow it into a meadow studded with old apple trees along Chappel Run. At one point, the trail goes right to the edge of the run, and this may have been a crossing site. But there has been a relocation, and you bear left into the woods again. At 5.8 miles (9.3 km) you cross Briggs Run, and then turn left for a short climb to another pipe-line swath. Turn right on this swath and follow it through a small clearing and then into another meadow with more old apple trees. Bear right off the pipe line and follow a succession of new trails and old roads to a meadow where you cross under a double wooden-poled power line at 6.7 miles (10.7 km). Soon you come to the bridge across Chappel Run. The bridge is a single log, but a steel cable has been rigged above to enable you to keep your balance. You then turn upstream a bit before turning right on a dirt road that takes you directly to the trailhead parking on PA 321.

You can hike farther along the North Country Trail. The trail continues south across PA 321 and climbs over the hill to cross PA 321 again near Red Bridge camping area, a distance of about six miles. It continues north of PA 59 to Sugar Run, about five more miles. The Rimrock-Morrison loop trail is about two miles west on PA 59. (Hike 26).

25

Chapman State Park

Distance: 7.0 miles (11.2 km)
Time: 4 hours
Rise: 840 feet (255 m)
Highlight: View
Maps: USGS 7½' Cherry Grove, Warren;
    state park map

Chapman State Park is a pleasant little park (only 800 acres) on the West Branch of Tionesta Creek near Warren. It is bordered by Allegheny National Forest, State Game Land 29 and a couple of tracts of private land. Although the park's trails are unusually well developed and extend onto the adjoining public lands, timber sales and oil and gas wells frequently disrupt the trail system. It is continuously being relocated and rebuilt.

At the time of my visit, a timber sale involved part of the yellow-blazed Adams Run Trail. All the trees to be cut had been blazed yellow, too, and the trail dissolved in a sea of blazes. That section has been avoided on this hike, but there may be other changes by the time of your visit. The state does not own the oil, gas or mineral rights under Chapman Park. Although one group of owners has volunteered not to exercise their rights until the twenty-first century, another group has already planned its first well just outside the park. If this well produces, up to 200 more wells will be drilled, many of them probably within the park. That the state does not own

the OGM rights under its own land is not at all unusual. Even the federal government owns only one to two percent of these rights in the 500,000-acre Allegheny National Forest.

Chapman Park is at the end of a paved but rough road leading west out of Clarendon on US 6 between Warren and Sheffield. From the turn at the traffic light, it is 5.0 miles to the picnic area parking lot just below the dam where this hike begins. Ordinary walking shoes should suffice, but there are wet spots.

Cross the park road to the Penny Run Trail, squeeze around the gate, cross the bridge and start up the trail marked with blue plastic diamonds nailed to the trees. This trail was rebuilt by the Youth Conservation Corps in 1980 and mostly uses old roads. It climbs first through open woods on a smooth old road to 0.4 mile (0.6 km) where it diverges left to avoid some wet spots. It then returns to the old road and continues to 0.6 mile (0.9 km) where it turns right across a bridge and continues to a corner of Allegheny National Forest. Here you turn right and follow another old road to

Ladder up Big Rock

the corner of a fern patch where you again turn right and descend along yet another old road. At 1.1 miles (1.7 km) you cross a bridge over Penny Run and continue to 1.4 miles (2.2 km) where you again turn right to reach the park road.

Turn left along the park road and follow it to 1.7 miles (2.7 km), where you pass a vehicle gate and head up the Lumber Trail. Because the Lumber Trail doubles as a snowmobile trail in winter, a problem in marking obscures the turnoff from this trail. The turn is at 1.9 miles (3.0 km) and to the right. The sign is hidden behind a pair of old apple trees; all you can see from your side is a snowmobile logo. The water tank is still visible up the hill behind you. Turn right onto the Nature Trail, blazed with white T's, and follow it downhill through a hemlock grove. At the bottom you cross a stream on a bridge and then turn upstream to circle the upper campground loop. On the far side of this loop, the trail passes through several campsites and is in need of relocation. (A troop of Girl Scouts was scheduled to work on the Nature Trail the week after I was there.) At 2.4 miles (3.9 km) you turn sharply left on another loop of the Nature Trail that skirts the lower campground loop and leads to a junction with the Gamelands Trail at 2.8 miles (4.5 km). This trail is the bed of the old Tionesta Valley Railroad. Turn left on it.

Soon the Lowlands Trail diverges to

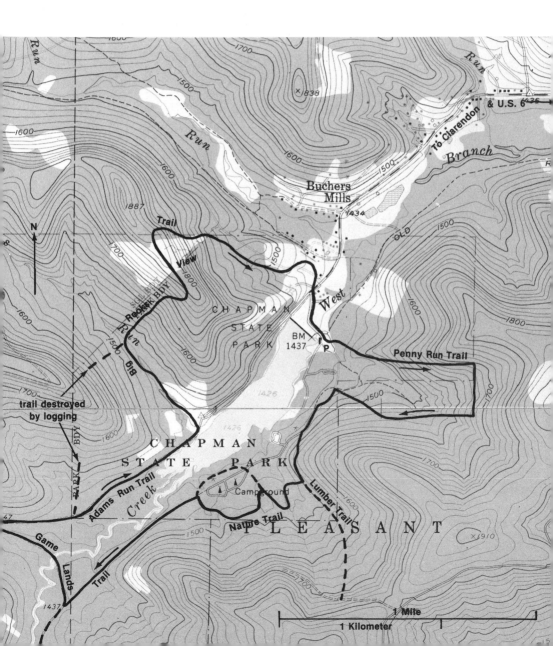

the right, and you can see the swing bridge it uses to cross the West Branch of Tionesta Creek. But you continue ahead on the old railroad grade to 3.4 miles (5.5 km) where you bear right and quickly come to the dirt road through State Game Land 29. Turn right on this road and follow it through the lowlands, where you see black cherry, white pine, service berry and lots of fern as well as hemlock, aspen, and an occasional apple tree. Wherever the loggers worked or rode, you still find these old apple trees. Apples were the only fruit the loggers ate. The old apple trees you see today are the result of the cores they tossed away.

Next you cross the West Branch and continue to 3.9 miles (6.3 km) where the dirt road makes a sharper than 90 degree turn to the right. Soon you are back to the border of Chapman State Park where the Adams Run Trail goes up the hill. Continue on the management road past the Lowlands Trail to the vehicle gate at the parking lot for group camping. Note the wood duck boxes on posts out in the lake.

Cross Adams Run on the road, and then turn left along the lower edge of the ski, sled and toboggan hill. At the far corner of the clearing you pick up the red-blazed Big Rocks Trail and the yellow-blazed Adams Run Trail as they follow an old railroad grade up the valley. Soon you cross Adams Run, and at 5.4 miles (8.6 km) you turn right on the Big Rocks Trail, cross Adams Run again and climb the hill. You are following the boundary of Game Land 29, and soon you reach the corner of a recently logged area. Note the abundance of black cherry seedlings along the trail.

As the hill grows steeper, you swing away from the boundary but quickly return and enter the clearcut to reach the big rocks. One large boulder to the right of the trail has a ladder up the side. The ladder is firmly anchored in place, and from the top you get a long view down the valley of the West Branch.

Back on the trail, you dodge closely around the base of a shelter rock before you finally swing down the side of the hill. It will take your best trail sense to follow this route as there are no blazes anywhere in the clearcut, except for one at shelter rock.

Turn right on the red-blazed Big Rocks Trail only when you can see the forestry road ahead. The trail parallels the road and reenters the state park. At 6.3 miles (10.0 km) you cross a motorcycle trail at a mudhole. After threatening to cross the road several times, the Big Rocks Trail finally does so and then swings through a plantation of red and white pine, passing very close to the border of some private land. At 6.6 miles (10.6 km) you jog left on the road and then cut across a corner of land in front of the park office. Cross the road and follow the park road below the dam. Use the footbridge to cross the West Branch. On the far side you are back at the picnic area parking lot and your car.

Much of the Elkhorn Run hiking trail has been destroyed by oil drilling. The opportunities for further hiking at Chapman State Park are limited to the management road through the game lands and the Lumber Trail. Check at the park office for other trails that may have been opened.

Rimrock-Morrison Trail

Distance: 9.5 miles (15.2 km)
Time: 5¼ hours
Rise: 1,020 feet (310 m)
Highlights: Mountain stream and waterfalls
Map: USGS 7½' Cornplanter Bridge

Rimrock-Morrison Trail is a circuit trail in Allegheny National Forest between PA 59 and the Kinzua arm of Allegheny Reservoir. It was laid out and cleared by the Allegheny Outdoor Club. Originally blazed as an 11.5 mile loop with a cutoff, the eastern part of the loop has been closed for logging. By using the Morrison campground, roughly halfway around, this hike could be turned into a two day backpack. But leaving a car on PA 59 overnight is not advisable. The trailhead is located on the south side of the highway, 4.3 miles west of PA 321 and the Bradford ranger station and 0.8 mile east of the road to Rimrock Overlook. Because of the many wet spots and the rocky trail, hiking boots are in order.

Start your hike by following the blue "eye" blazes south away from the highway. After a couple of stream crossings, you pass through an open meadow with ferns and some old apple trees at 0.6 mile (1.0 km). At 0.7 mile (1.1 km) you reach the loop junction and turn right, climbing a bit to regain the plateau. The trail here is cut through thickets of mountain laurel. In most years, the laurel blooms in the last week of June. The best displays are

usually those patches exposed to direct sunlight. Service berries, some of them good-sized trees, are also found along this section. At 1.5 miles (2.4 km) turn left on an old logging road. This begins a particularly pleasant section of the hike. A clearing to the right of the trail is passed at 1.8 miles (2.9 km), and shortly you bear left. At 2.3 miles (3.7 km) you turn left at a fork in the old logging road, and soon you turn right onto the trail.

Along this section, look for the ghostly Indian pipe flower. The Indian pipe is a saprophyte. It lives on dead and decaying organic material, like a fungus. Along the stems you can see tiny vestigal leaves—totally devoid of chlorophyll.

At 2.9 miles (4.7 km) you start to descend into Campbell Run. Soon you cross a side stream and then continue among large conglomerate boulders. Conglomerate looks like concrete, but it is really a very coarse sandstone. Pebble-sized chunks of still older rocks have been cemented together.

A bit farther down the ravine the trail picks up an old road and follows it, except for a detour around a wet place. At 3.6 miles (5.7 km) you turn left off the old road and start to cut across the steep slope that drops into the reservoir below. Here, the trail passes among some large hemlocks. You can hear power boats on the reservoir even though you can't see them. At 3.8 miles (6.1 km) you can see the reservoir through the trees as you cross an old log skid. Log skids were troughs, lubricated with oil or ice, used to slide logs downhill.

Next you bear left on another old road and climb far up the slope on it. Along the way you pass a white pine. Farther up you cross a couple of streams and then bear right off the old road onto the trail which passes among more large boulders.

At 4.4 miles (7.0 km) you cross a stream at the edge of a meadow and then continue on a more recent logging road. Soon you come to a view of the reservoir from the top of a large conglomerate boulder, but the view could

Morrison Run

be much improved if a single black birch were removed.

At 4.7 miles (7.5 km) bear left off the logging road past some dogwoods and continue across the slope on rough trail. Along this stretch you pass a pair of white pines. You cross another old log skid at 5.1 miles (8.2 km), and again you can see the water below, through the trees. At 5.5 miles (8.9 km) you reach the corner of a meadow with a view of the reservoir. As you continue along the edge of the meadow you pass old apple trees and high bush blueberry. The trail then enters the meadow, and you see crab apples and hawthorns growing here, as well as some spruce that have been planted.

At 5.8 miles (9.2 km) you cross a trail that leads to Morrison campground. Your trail now begins to swing upstream along Morrison Run, crossing a couple of side streams, and then picks up an old road. A critical turn is reached at 6.3 miles (10.1 km) where you turn sharp right off the old road and drop down to Morrison Run. At the run, you move upstream, staying on the west side. (Camping is also permitted a short way up Morrison Run.) You continue upstream, sometimes following what appears to be an old railroad grade to 7.6 miles (12.2 km), where you come to the Forks of the Morrison, in a small meadow. If the eastern part of the loop is still closed, you must turn up the left fork here. Almost immediately, you cross the left fork, and soon you step across it again. Climbing along the left fork is steeper than the main stream.

Soon you notice small waterfalls in the stream below, and then you come to a mini-glen. The Morrison has saved the best for the last. Giant boulders have slid into the stream here, forming waterfalls. Soon you cross the left fork again and then climb steeply through some more large boulders to an old road at 8.3 miles (13.2 km). Turn left and continue to the last crossing of the left fork, and shortly beyond, you reach the loop junction at 8.8 miles (14.1 km). Follow the access trail back to PA 59 and the trailhead.

The best bet for further hiking in this part of the woods is the North Country Trail that crosses PA 59 two miles to the east. (See Hike 24.)

27

Tracy Ridge Trail

Distance: 10.3 miles (16.7 km)
Time: 5½ hours
Rise: 1,200 feet (360 m)
Highlight: North Country Trail
Maps: USGS 7½' Cornplanter Run, Stickney;
   Hiker's Guide to Allegheny National Forest, map 1

Another large roadless area in Allegheny National Forest is Tracy Ridge in the northern part of the forest, just south of the New York border. The area is bounded by PA 321 on the east, Willow Bay Recreational Area on the north, Allegheny Reservoir on the west and Sugar Bay on the south. Tracy Ridge has been proposed for National Recreation Area status:

This hike is a daylong circuit, following parts of the Johnnycake and North Country trails as well as Tracy Ridge Trail. Despite some wet spots and the length of the hike, it could probably be done with good walking shoes, at least during the drier times of the year. The hike could be turned into a two day backpack by using the Handsome Lake campground, south of Johnnycake Run on the North Country Trail. But it is not advisable to leave cars overnight at the trailhead on PA 321, and the Tracy Ridge campground is open only on Memorial Day, July Fourth and Labor Day weekends.

The Tracy Ridge Trail parking lot is on the west side of PA 321, 2.6 miles south of the junction with PA 346, 0.4 mile north of the entrance to Tracy Ridge campground, and 11.0 miles north of the junction with PA 59.

Step over the log restricting access to an old fire road and start your hike on the Tracy Ridge Trail. At 0.2 mile (0.3 km) turn left on the trail that's blue-blazed. The so-called "eye" blazes, popular in Allegheny National Forest, are used here. These blazes consist of a small horizontal rectangle over a larger vertical rectangle. When done correctly on reasonably smooth bark, they resemble a block letter "i." They do avoid confusion with trees marked for sale but create problems at turns and intersections. There used to be trail signs at all of these points, but half or more of them were missing at the time of my trip.

At. 0.5 mile (0.8 km) bear right where the first of several unmarked side trails leads toward Tracy Ridge campground. Partway past some big rocks at 0.8 mile (1.2 km), the trail turns sharply left and proceeds through a narrow passage. The campground is visible through the trees. Beyond the rocks, you bear right and continue to an old jeep road at 1.0 mile (1.6 km) where you jog right. You reach the Johnnycake Trail junction at

To PA 346

Run

N

1900

2100

× 2201

2100

2200

2200

2100

2200

JOHNNYCAKE TR. P BM 2214

Tracy Ridge
Campground

Nelse

Run

321

Interpretive Trail

TRAIL

2100

2000

D O N

2200

2000

41

To PA 59

2000

1.4 miles (2.2 km). You will return on the Johnnycake Trail to this point. But now bear right and continue on Tracy Ridge. Tracy Ridge is broad and flat, so you don't begin to see its edge until you are well along. As the ridge narrows, you swing over the left side to start down to Allegheny Reservoir. This is a new trail, built to avoid a steep drop down the ridge line itself. Soon you swing back to the ridge line and continue to descend.

At 4.2 miles (6.7 km) and the bottom of the hill, you reach a junction with the white-blazed North Country Trail. To your right, the North Country Trail leads to Allegany State Park in New York. Yes, there is a different spelling on the other side of the state line. The reservoir can be seen through the trees. The North Country Trail cuts across the steep hillside that drops into the reservoir. Keep an eye out for high bush blueberry. They probably never bear much under the trees, but you might find a few berries in July.

Along the hillside you cross a number of streams of various sizes. Whisky Run is the largest of these, and you cross it at 5.9 miles (9.4 km). At 6.3 miles (10.1 km) you pass through an open grove of white pine. The North Country Trail now swings eastward in order to round Johnnycake Run inlet on the reservoir. Johnnycake Trail and run are reached at 6.6 miles (10.6 km). The North Country Trail crosses the run and continues to Handsome Lake campground and, eventually, to North Dakota. But you turn left and follow the blue-blazed Johnnycake Trail upstream.

At 7.1 miles (11.4 km) note evidence of an old corduroy road at a side stream crossing. Johnnycake Run itself is crossed at 7.3 miles (11.7 km) and again at 7.6 miles (12.1 km). At 8.9 miles (14.2 km) you pass a junction with the Interpretive Trail on your right, and at the top of the hill you bear right on the Tracy Ridge Trail. From here you retrace your steps to your car.

This hike could be extended by following the North Country Trail either to the north or south. The only other hike appears to be the 2.5 mile Interpretive Trail around the campground.

28

Mill Creek Trail

Distance: 10.8 miles (17.3 km)
Time: 5½ hours
Rise: 880 feet (270 m)
Highlight: Kane Experimental Forest
Maps: USGS 7½' James City; PA Hiking Trails
   9th Ed., pg. 104

Mill Creek Trail is a large double-loop trail near the Twin Lakes Recreational Area, south of Kane. The Mill Creek Trail is quite new but uses parts of two older trails, Twin Lakes and Black Cherry. A connecting trail permits you to shorten the hike. Even so, this is a boot buster. There is a respectable amount of climbing, but it is widely distributed along this hike, with no single climb exceeding 200 feet.

The trailhead is on Forestry Road 191, which can be reached from PA 321 by turning west at a junction 2.9 miles north of the US 219 junction in Wilcox. A small sign at the junction says simply "Twin Lakes." This junction was the site of Dahoga, where a sawmill was located in the 1890's. Now it is just another ghost town in Penn's Woods. The trailhead is 2.0 miles up the forestry road. There is a sizeable parking lot in a bend on the right side of the road. There is an outhouse but no water at this spot. A sign indicates the start of the trail but gives the distance around the short loop as only nine miles. This may be only the distance to the junction with the Twin Lakes Trail. The distance

around the long loop is probably also underestimated. The Mill Creek Trail is marked with Allegheny National Forest yellow "eye" blazes. Due to the length of this hike and the presence of some wet spots, hiking boots are preferable, but you might get away with good walking shoes.

The trail climbs away from the forestry road and then turns left briefly on a pipeline before emerging at the edge of a clearcut at the top of the hill. Here you jog left and then turn sharply right to follow a logging road across the clearcut. You reach the far edge of the clearcut at 0.5 mile (0.8 km) and continue into deep woods. The edge of the clearcut appears to be the boundary of the Kane Experimental Forest. Experiments in silviculture are carried out here. Silviculture is the growing of trees as a crop. Superior strains are planted and thinning and cutting schemes employed to improve the yields of timber and pulpwood. Next you cross a stream on a log bridge, and at 1.0 mile (1.6 km) you cross Forestry Road 123.

As you walk quietly through the forest in the early morning you may be rewarded with a view of a large hawk as it wings its way silently between the trees. It's hard to believe that such large birds can make so little noise when they fly. Soon you pass a spring to the left of the trail, and at 1.8 miles (2.8 km) you cross Forestry Road 138. Black cherry, a northern hardwood used in furniture and paneling, is abundant along much of the trail. By the time you cross the wide swath of a Tenneco natural gas pipe line at 2.1 miles (3.4 km) you have left the Kane Experimental Forest. You have an opportunity here to compare the heat in the open swath to the cooler and moister conditions under the forest canopy. The contrast is particularly dramatic on a hot sunny day.

Beyond the swath, the trail follows some older and smaller pipe lines.

Sometimes the pipes are right on the surface. The trail enters a spooky hemlock hollow bordering Wolf Run, which you cross as best you can. You cross a jeep road, which is an extension of Forestry Road 334. The trail climbs gently up the side of the valley and follows the edge of Wolf Run Valley for the next several kilometers. As you approach the connecting trail junction, the woods are very open, and you can see a telephone line that follows the broad ridge between Wolf Run and Big Mill Creek. You reach this junction at 3.7 miles (5.9 km). The long loop goes off to the left, but you continue straight on and soon enter a recently-lumbered area that appears to be coming back to black cherry and beech. Here the trail is marked with blazed posts, and so thick is the new forest that it is

Mill Creek Trail

sometimes hard to see from one post to the next.

At 4.0 miles (6.4 km) you cross under the telephone line you saw earlier and continue to a crossing of Forestry Road 185 at a junction with Forestry Road 239. Forestry Road 185 is part of the Highland Hills Scenic Drive. You follow road 239, which is also marked with blazed posts. At 4.6 miles (7.3 km) you continue ahead on a jeep road where Forestry Road 239 turns left, and soon you climb over a pile of earth, which obviously has not been effective in stopping vehicles. Then you pass a large rock, sliding slowly toward Big Mill Creek. You pass a sand pit and, just beyond it, a spring to the right of the trail.

At 5.1 miles (8.2 km) your reach the junction with the long loop of Mill Creek Trail from the left. You continue ahead toward Twin Lakes on the old road you've been following. You turn right onto trail at 5.3 miles (8.5 km) and climb above the road. At 6.1 miles (9.7 km) you cross a stream, and soon you see a large clearcut area to your left. At times the trail goes right up to the edge of the clearcut but then veers back into the cool woods again. Next you pick up a logging road in the middle of a small clearing and follow it for a bit before turning left onto a trail. Soon you see spruce growing along the trail, apparently the result of an under planting. The spruce tolerate shade, grow slowly and may eventually burst through the forest canopy to take over. The large clearcut can still be seen to the left in places.

At 6.8 miles (10.9 km) you cross the wide Tenneco gas pipe line swath and continue through an evergreen plantation of red pine and Norway spruce. At 7.4 miles (11.9 km) you again cross the white-blazed boundary of the Kane Experimental Forest and soon pass through several clearings. Jog right across one jeep road at 8.1 miles (12.9 km) and soon jog left across another. Here you enter an area of old-growth beech with a few sugar maples. Presumably the hemlocks were cut out of this stand long ago. Beechwood is brittle and may shatter while being sawed, and this may account for its survival here.

At 8.4 miles (13.4 km) you reach the blue-blazed Twin Lakes Trail and turn right. Immediately you cross Forestry Road 138 and continue through more large beech trees. You cross the white-blazed Kane Experimental Forest boundary for the last time at 8.6 miles (13.8 km) and soon cross Forestry Road 331. Shortly beyond, you jog right across a woods road. At 8.9 miles (14.3 km) you pass under the telephone line again and re-cross Forestry Road 331. Forestry Road 331 is crossed for the last time at 9.3 miles (14.9 km) and soon you bear left on an old road and start to descend towards Hoffman Run and Twin Lakes Recreation Area. At 9.7 miles (15.5 km) you come to the end of the Twin Lakes Trail at a junction with the Black Cherry Trail. Turn left on the Black Cherry and shortly bear left again. Be sure to take time to read the markers along this trail. They are unusually informative. Farther along, you cross a small stream repeatedly, but always on bridges. At 10.4 miles (16.6 km) you turn right on the paved Forestry Road 191. No parking is permitted here, so you have to walk back on the road, passing the campground roads, a road to the beach area and the far end of the Black Cherry Trail before reaching the parking lot and your car.

Other hikes in the Twin Lakes Area include the long loop of Mill Creek Trail, which is suitable for a two-day backpack, the western parts of the Twin Lakes Trail and the balance of the Black Cherry Trail.

Hickory Creek Trail

Distance: 11.6 miles (18.7 km)
Time: 7 hours
Rise: 1,030 feet (315 meters)
Highlights: Large roadless area, old logging
   camp
Maps: USGS 7½' Cobham; U.S. Forest Service
   map

Hickory Creek Trail is located within a large roadless area in Allegheny National Forest. The trail is contained in the wedge of land between East Hickory and Middle Hickory creeks. Hickory Creek has been proposed for wilderness status. Although roadless today, the area was not always so. Nearly every valley contains the bed of a logging railroad, while old skid roads and more recent jeep trails lace the hillsides. The area was logged by Wheeler and Dusenbury of Endeavor, starting around 1910. This company lumbered in Pennsylvania and New York for over a century, starting in 1837.

Instead of doing Hickory Creek as a long day hike, many people prefer to turn it into a backpack of two or more days. With just a daypack you can probably shave an hour or more off the hiking time, but backpackers will need the full seven hours on the trail.

The trailhead is at Hearts Content Picnic Area. Hearts Content is most easily reached from PA 337 at a junction 10.1 miles from PA 62 at Tidioute and 11.4 miles from US 6 at Warren. Turn south on the Hearts Content-Sheffield Road (LR 61031). Signs at this junction refer only to Sheffield. Another 3.7 miles brings you to the trailhead. Drinking water is available at the picnic area during the summer. Yellow blazes consisting of a large vertical rectangle surmounted by a smaller horizontal rectangle are used to mark the Hickory Creek Trail. Despite the length of the trail and some wet spots, you could get by with walking shoes.

The trail quickly traverses a red pine plantation and then crosses the road leading to Hearts Content. On the far side of the road it passes under the junction of two pole lines and joins the loop at 0.6 mile (1.0 km) from the start. Turn left through characteristically open woods. The very openness of the woods forces you to keep a sharp lookout for the blazes, as the footway fades out frequently. But the footing is fairly even and the walking easy as you swing along generally downhill. You cross a woods road at 0.8 mile (1.3 km) and pass a spring to the right at 1.1 miles (1.7 km). At 1.5 miles (2.4 km) you cross a nameless tributary of Middle Hickory Creek on a log bridge, and immediately beyond you cross an old logging road. You begin a gradual climb at 1.9 miles

(3.1 km), and at the top you pass through an open area abounding in ferns. The trail continues gently up and down as it follows the edge of the plateau. Trees along this stretch are black cherry, beech, maple, red oak and hemlock. Just beyond 3.5 miles (5.6 km) you cross an old road and a dry watercourse and then bear left on another old road for a stretch. A large meadow along Coon Run is reached at 3.9 miles (6.2 km). You then cross a tributary of Coon and head downstream along the edge of the meadow.

The meadows along Coon Run offer the first opportunities for camping, and you will see several campsites along the trail. You cross Coon Run itself at 4.4 miles (7.0 km) and immediately cross the bed of a fine old logging railroad. Note the parallel depressions across the grade where the uncreosoted ties rotted in place. These depressions are one of the surest signs of an old railroad grade. Old railroad grades can be hard to identify as most of them were never mapped. This one appears to have been standard gauge.

You now move upstream for 200 yards before diverging from the stream and starting the gradual climb into the next watershed. At 5.4 miles (8.6 km) you cross an open swath leading to a meadow on your right and shortly jog left across an old road. You cross a couple of streams at 5.8 miles (9.3 km) and then continue past a large meadow to your right. Another tree growing here is yellow birch. Soon you are following an old logging railroad grade along Jacks Run. There are more opportunities for camping along this stream.

The ruins of an old logging camp can be found along Jacks Run. The camp was of unusual design in that it was all under one roof, like a railroad flat. Iron work from school desks was found here. Was there once a small school in

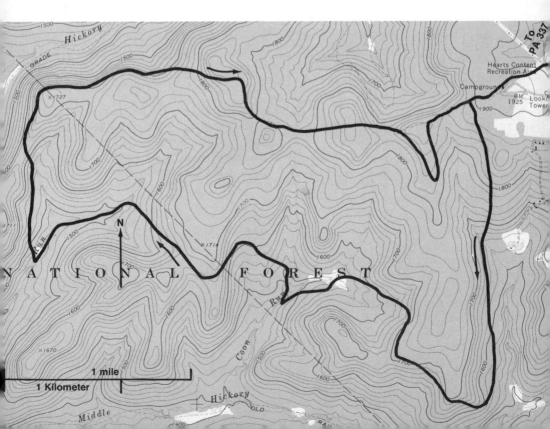

Meadow

the midst of this now roadless area?

There are only a couple of stream crossings as the trail follows Jacks Run for about 0.6 mile (1 km). At the last crossing, turn right and start the gentle climb to the broad ridge between East and Middle Hickory creeks.

At a saddle 7.0 miles (11.2 km) in the ridge the trail switches to the far side and continues to climb, reaching the top of the hill at 7.4 miles (11.9 km). There should be some leaves-off views over the valley of East Hickory Creek from this section.

At 7.8 miles (12.5 km) you cross a small stream, and at 8.3 miles (13.3 km) you swing away from the edge of the ridge, cross another small stream, and start to climb again. You now swing right, along the base of a slope, and

climb among large boulders. At 8.8 miles (14.0 km) you are back to an edge that drops off to the left. You cross a jeep trail at 9.1 miles (14.6 km), a small meadow at 9.5 miles (15.2 km), and another old railroad grade at 10 miles (16.0 km). These landmarks are followed by a woods road at 10.4 miles (16.6 km), and at 11.1 miles (17.7 km) you are back at the loop junction. Turn left, and it is 0.6 mile (1.0 km) back to the trailhead and your car.

Other hikes in the Hearts Content vicinity are to be found on the nearby Tanbark Trail and some shorter trails. Two circuit hikes, using the Tanbark Trail, are described in Hikes 19 and 21. A very short hike in the Hearts Content Scenic Area is described in Hike 17.

30

Tionesta Scenic Area

Distance: 11.8 miles (18.9 km)
Time: 6 hours
Rise: 1,080 feet (330 m)
Highlights: Large stand of virgin timber; relics
  of the Petroleum Age
Maps: USGS 7½' Ludlow, Sheffield; Hiker's
  Guide to Allegheny National Forest, map 5

In 1934, with the help of the Pennsylvania Forestry Association, the United States Forest Service bought 4,070 acres of virgin timber southeast of Sheffield. This tract was divided into two parts of roughly equal size. The Tionesta Scenic Area is open to the public and is traversed by the North Country and Twin Lakes trails as well as some other trails. The other 2,000 acres is the Tionesta Natural Area, which is used strictly for research, to monitor the changes of a mature and unmanaged forest. But a natural gas storage field is located beneath the area. Over seven miles of this boot-buster hike are within or along the boundary of the Scenic Area.

The trailhead is on PA 948, 5.3 miles south of the intersection with US 6 in Sheffield. The North Country Trail crossing is signed, and there is parking for several cars along the east side of the highway, where this hike begins. Because of the length of this hike, as well as many wet spots and seven crossings of Cherry Run, hiking boots are strongly recommended.

To start, head east into the woods

along the white-"eye"-blazed North Country Trail and descend gently to the south branch of Tionesta Creek. At 0.3 mile (0.5 km) you turn left on Forest Road 148 and cross the creek on the road bridge. Bypass the first crossroad and then bear left on Forest Road 446. Turn right into the woods along Cherry Run and follow the blazes carefully. The woods are very open, and the footway is not well established. At 0.8 mile (1.2 km) you pass the ruins of an old railway caboose that appears to have had a second life as a cabin. Soon you cross

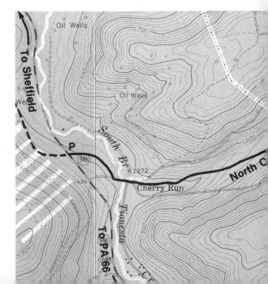

Cherry Run on stepping stones, and almost immediately, the footway becomes easier to follow. At 1.4 miles (2.3 km) you cross a large power line swath, and soon you cross Cherry Run again and pass among old oil wells. Not only do you discover the history of Penn's Woods on this hike, but you also see rusting relics of the Petroleum Age.

Cherry Run is crossed a third time at 1.7 miles (2.7 km). You then dodge around an old apple tree and begin climbing an old road. At 2.1 miles (3.4 km) the boundary of the Tionesta Scenic Area is marked by a display case, and at 2.3 miles (3.7 km) you bear

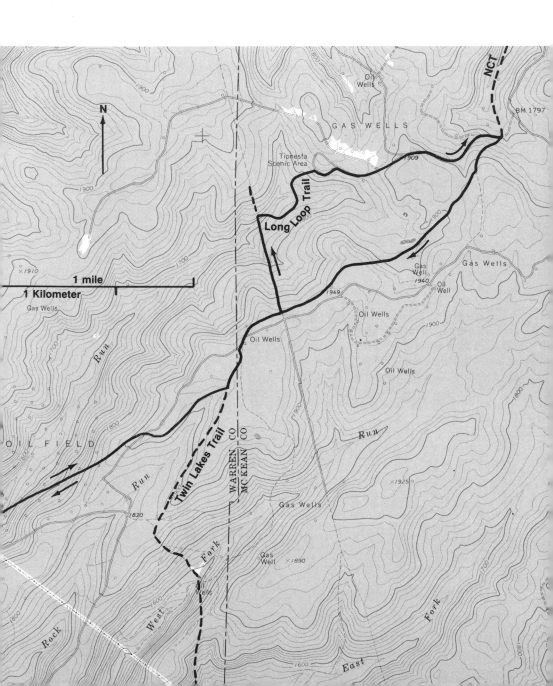

left off the grade through very open woods. Every so often you encounter old pipes that once collected oil from wells now gone dry. The most common trees here are large black cherries. Next, the trail threads its way among large sandstone boulders, and even here there is an old pipe line between the rocks. At 2.9 miles (4.7 km) you reach the top of the hill and cross a dirt road. Continuing on trails and old roads, you reach the junction with the blue-"eye"-blazed Twin Lakes Trail at 3.2 miles (5.1 km). This is one of the major trail junctions in Allegheny National Forest. The somewhat confusing distance sign on the North Country Trail predates 1975, when this section was still the Tanbark Trail. The North Country Trail does not go to Hearts Content, and it will be a lot more than 29 miles when the North Country Trail finally is extended to the Allegheny river. Turn left on the white blazes and follow them out to 3.5 miles (5.6 km) where you turn right on a dirt road. You soon turn left and pass a more recent, but still abandoned, oil well.

At 3.8 miles (6.1 km) you reach the swath of a large pipe line. Turn left and follow it downhill to a crossing of a much shrunken Cherry Run. Start up the far side, and at 4.3 miles (6.9 km) turn right on the Long Loop Nature Trail. This unblazed but obvious trail takes you back across Cherry Run on a bridge and then winds slowly upward through large hemlocks, beech and black cherry trees. A red-tailed hawk skims the tree tops, screaming again and again, adding another wild note to this forest primeval. This is a nature trail and has many explanatory signs. It seems curious that such large trees have such tiny cones. A hemlock cone is only the size of the end of your little finger, but it contains many seeds. Hemlock seeds weigh two or three milligrams each.

Research has found that hobble-bush, the most common shrub in the 1940's, vanished by the early '50's. This change is attributed to heavy browsing by deer.

After crossing Cherry Run again on a bridge, you reach a junction with the Short Loop Trail. Bear right and you soon reach a forest road at 5.2 miles (8.3 km). Turn right and follow the dirt road along the scenic area boundary. Other roads come in from the left along your way, but at each junction you continue ahead. At 6.3 miles (10.0 km) you turn right on the North Country Trail and climb back to the top of the hill on a series of old roads and new trails. At one point, the trail follows an old pipe line through the woods, and at 8.0 miles (12.8 km) you reach the pipe line swath where you earlier turned off the North Country Trail. Continue ahead, retracing your steps on the North Country Trail to PA 948 and your car.

31

North Country Trail

Distance: 12.4 miles (20.0 km)
Time: 7 hours
Rise: 2,030 feet (620 m)
Highlights: Large roadless area; remnants
of the Petroleum Age
Maps: USGS 7½' Mayburg, Marienville West;
Hiker's Guide to the Allegheny National
Forest, maps 9, 10 and 11

One of the largest roadless areas in the Allegheny National Forest is between Kelletville and Marienville. It is known as the Salmon Creek area. It contains the longest stretch of the North Country Trail in Penn's Woods that does not cross a road. Salmon Creek is the least known of the large roadless areas in Allegheny National Forest and has not been proposed for wilderness status.

This hike is written as a day hike but could well be done as a two-day backpack. In either case, a simple car shuttle is involved. To reach the trailhead from PA 66 just west of Marienville, take the Muzette Road at the village of Roses. In 1.7 miles, just after crossing the national forest boundary, turn right on Forest Road 145. Another 1.2 miles brings you to Amsler Spring, an abandoned picnic area. The spring continues to flow, and there is parking at the edge of the road. Leave one car here and continue along Forest Road 145 for 7.3 miles to the junction with Forest Road 127, just outside of Kelletville. Turn right on Forest Road

127, and it is only 0.2 mile to the signed North Country Trail crossing. There is a pull-off on the left, just beyond the crossing, with space for a couple of cars. There is a little additional space back at the junction with Forest Road 145. The length of this hike—plus wet places, stream crossings and rocks—make hiking boots in order. White "eye" blazes are used to mark the North Country Trail.

To start the hike, follow the North Country Trail up the hill away from the road. Shortly you pass some large sand-stone boulders, and at 0.6 miles (0.9 km) the trail enters a recently logged area. Many of the blazed trees appear to be missing, and the footway is frequently covered with slash. Be very careful not to lose sight of one blaze before you can see another. Look on the back side of trees for blazes. At 1.0 mile (1.6 km) the trail leaves the logged area and passes among some very large boulders. Soon it reenters the logged area before reaching a more open part of the forest. Soon you reach the top of the hill and continue through open woods with lots of ferns, which make the trail easy to follow.

At 1.5 miles (2.4 km) you cross a logging road and continue past a large open area that appears to have been planted for wildlife. The trail descends gently down a side stream of Four Mile Run. At 2.6 miles (4.2 km) you turn left, cross the side stream and then cross a large meadow. Next you cross Four Mile Run itself and head up the next hill. Toward the top of the hill, pipes across the trail indicate that you have entered an old oil field. Soon you cross an old road to an oil well on your right. Next you can see a large metal building to your left. Steel rods radiate from this building to the various wells in the field. With these rods, a single large engine, running on natural gas, pumped all the wells in the field. You can see a similar system, in working order, at the Drake Well Museum near Titusville.

You cross a ridge line set about with big rocks at 4.1 miles (6.5 km) and then pass a shelter rock. The trail passes through open woods with many wild grape vines and then starts the descent into the next valley, a nameless tributary of Salmon Creek. At 4.9 miles (7.8 km) there is a very sharp switchback to the right onto an old road. Soon you turn left off the old road and switchback some more to a dry stream bed. At 5.4 miles (8.6 km) you turn left on a grassy road at the edge of a large meadow. You climb the next ridge on this road, passing a small sign that indicates a wildlife development area. At 5.7 miles (9.1 km) turn right at a split in the road, and soon you enter another meadow. Next turn left off the road, and soon the trail takes you along the edge of yet another meadow with views across Salmon Creek Valley. The trail then reenters the woods and starts down a nameless tributary of Guiton Run. There is good footing on this gentle descent.

The valley of Guiton Run makes a good campsite, if you are doing this

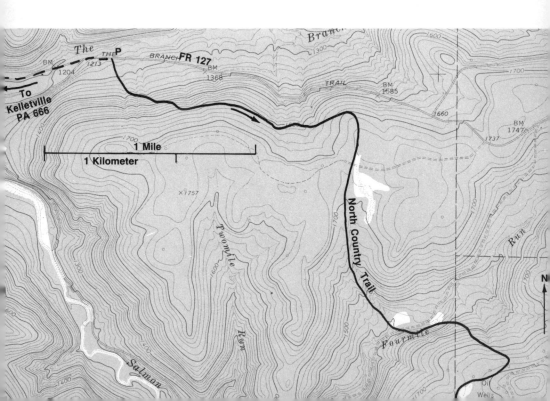

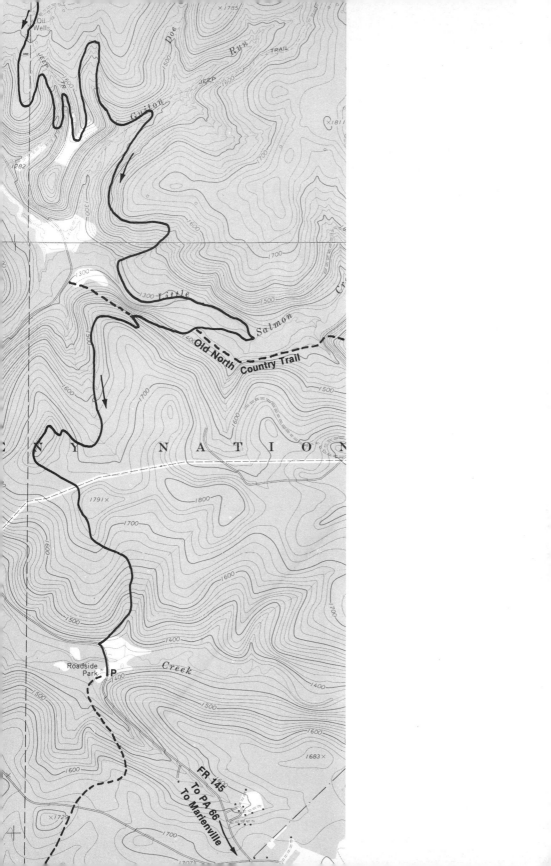

Author on
North Country Trail

hike as a two day backpack. The trail turns upstream along Guiton Run before crossing it at 7.1 miles (11.4 km). On the far side of Guiton, you climb through a meadow and then continue climbing for a bit after the trail reenters the woods. Next you turn right and descend across a meadow and a dry watercourse into the valley of Little Salmon Creek. At 8.1 miles (13.0 km) you turn left and proceed upstream along the Little Salmon on an old logging railroad grade along the edge of a meadow. The railroad belonged to the Salmon Creek Lumber Company, which

At 8.9 miles (14.2 km) you finally cross the Little Salmon on a log bridge of remarkable design. The bridge consists of two logs flattened on top with a railing down the middle. On the far side, the trail continues upstream for a bit before finally turning right. Soon you are back in the woods, and at 9.5 miles (15.2 km) you bear left at a fork where the old North Country Trail went ahead to Forest Road 145. The trail then

zigzags up the hill, crossing an old road along the way. Next you turn left up a small valley to 10.3 miles (16.5 km) where you turn right and cross the stream. After crossing a dry watercourse you turn right and pass some large rocks. Soon you turn left to reach the top of the hill where you turn right to an overhanging rock. Unfortunately, the overhang is set about with large trees so there is no view.

At 11.4 miles (18.2 km) you cross a pipe line swath and then climb a small hill to a clearing. Just beyond, you turn left and start down, passing some large rocks. At 12.2 miles (19.5 km) you bear right, leaving the watercourse and entering a meadow. Look for signs of beaver in this meadow. Many aspens have been cut down and dragged away. Turn left on Forest Road 145 and cross Salmon Creek on the road bridge. Note the beaver dam across Salmon Creek, just upstream from the bridge. Continue briefly along the road, and you are back to your car at Amsler Spring.

Pittsburgh and
the Southwest

32

Wolf Creek Narrows Natural Area

Distance: 1.5 miles (2.4 km)
Time: 1 hour
Rise: 140 feet (43 m)
Highlight: Spring wild flowers
Maps: USGS 7½' Slippery Rock; Western
   Pennsylvania Conservancy brochure map

Wolf Creek Narrows, near Slippery Rock in Butler County, is one of the most recent acquisitions of the Western Pennsylvania Conservancy. When I first visited the area, I had to cross a piece of private land, between the road and the Conservancy tract, that was open to Conservancy members only. Three months later, the Conservancy made another purchase so the trail to Wolf Creek Narrows Natural Area is now open to the public. Wolf Creek has its headwaters in Pine Swamp Natural Area, another Conservancy holding (See Hike 44).

The big attraction of Wolf Creek Narrows is its wild flowers in late April and early May. The ground is carpeted with them. You also get the best views of the creek before the trees leaf out. Laying out trails in a new natural area is painful, since you can't avoid destroying some of the wild flowers you are trying to save. But it has to be done. Without established trails, "horde paths" might well destroy even more.

Fiddleheads

The trailhead for Wolf Creek Narrows is 1.7 miles west of PA 258 in Slippery Rock, on West Water Street. Cross the bridge over Wolf Creek and take the first left at the sign: "Slippery Rock State College No Trespassing." Parking is permitted just inside the fringe of trees along the road, but please don't block the lane and don't park along the road. Ordinary walking shoes should be fine for this short hike.

To start, walk back across the bridge and turn left on the unmarked but obvious trail at the end of the bridge abutment. This trail takes you upstream along Wolf Creek into the bulk of the Natural Area. Beware of disturbing any logs along this trail. On my visits, one of the logs contained a nest of hornets, which swarmed to the attack when disturbed. At 0.3 mile (0.4 km) you encounter the first white blazes. Keep a sharp eye out for the loop trail junction where you turn right and follow the trail across the bottom land to the base of the hill. Many of the best wild flowers are found on the south slope of the hill. Partway up, the orange-blazed Hepatica Trail goes off to the left. Trees growing

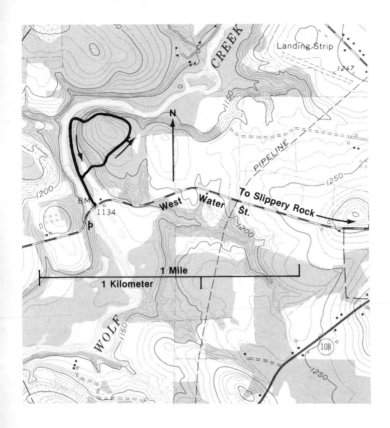

on the slope are black cherry, hemlock, beech, maple and basswood. In late April, abundant wild flowers are hepatica, may apple and trillium. At 0.6 mile (1.0 km) you turn left above the narrows. Glimpses of Wolf Creek can be seen between the trees. Soon you reach the edge of the hill and descend to the creek, which runs on bedrock at this point. Another tree found here is black gum. The trail continues along the edge of the stream and under the hemlocks, with views of the small cliffs in the limestone on the far side. At 1.2 miles (1.9 km) you close the loop trail and retrace your steps to your car.

The conservancy tract includes an area on the far side of Wolf Creek. It has no marked trails and can be reached only by fording the creek. The Jennings Nature Reserve, on the other side of Slippery Rock, at the junction of PA 8 and PA 173, offers additional trails and wild flowers. (See Hike 34.)

Todd Sanctuary

Distance: 2.1 miles (3.4 km)
Time: 1½ hours
Rise: 240 feet (75 m)
Highlights: Spring wild flowers, birds
Maps: USGS 7½' Freeport; Nature Trail map

Todd Sanctuary consists of 160 acres along Watson Run in the southeast corner of Butler County. Owned and operated by the Audubon Society of Western Pennsylvania, it is named for the late W.E. Clyde Todd, curator of the bird section in the Carnegie Museum of Natural History. Todd spent his boyhood summers near here and began a detailed study of the bird population over 70 years ago. At least 214 species of birds have been observed here, so be sure to bring your binoculars. Todd Sanctuary dates back to 1942, making it one of the first natural areas to be preserved in the vicinity of Pittsburgh. This delightful short hike is designed to take you through all the different habitats in the sanctuary. It would be particularly suitable for small children as there are lots of things to see and discover, including some blackberries in season. There are also many opportunities to shorten the hike. Spring wild flowers include bloodroot, trailing arbutus, trillium, spring beauty, dutchman's breeches and forget-me-not. The best displays are in the bottom lands along Watson Run. The trails are ex-

cellent, so ordinary walking shoes are fine.

To reach Todd Sanctuary from Pittsburgh, take new PA 28 and turn north on PA 356. In 1.0 mile turn east on Monroe Road, across from Cinema 356. After crossing the railroad tracks and going up a steep hill, bear right at a fork in the road. This is Kepple Road, which takes you past a golf course to reach the Todd Sanctuary sign 3.0 miles from PA 356. Turn right into the parking lot. The insects are said never to get too bad at Todd.

The hike starts at the bulletin board in the corner of the parking lot. Follow the trail and turn right on the road paralleling Knixon's Run. After 400 feet turn left at McCray Crossing, a footbridge over Hesselgesser's Run, to the cabin where you will usually find a naturalist or two in residence. A recycled birdhouse at the cabin will receive your contribution, which is needed for the sanctuary's support. A guest register is maintained here, and there are usually several informal exhibits. Drinking water is available.

Bear right around the cabin and then

go left on the Loop Trail. Soon you turn left where the Warbler Trail goes ahead. At 0.4 mile (0.6 km) you pass an old limestone quarry to the left of the trail, where much of the stone to build the cabin was obtained. Shortly you bear left where the Warbler Trail comes in from the right. At 0.6 mile (0.9 km) you cross Watson Run, just before the Indian Pipe Trail goes off to the right. Next you bear left on the Loop Trail where the Pond Trail goes ahead. Soon you emerge at the edge of the pond, which was built in 1969 to attract migrating water birds. As you continue through the meadow around the pond, there is a large white farmhouse to your left. This is the farmhouse, belonging to his grandfather, where W.E. Clyde Todd spent his boyhood summers.

Trees along the Loop Trail are shingle oak, red oak, white oak, crab apple, black gum, scotch pine, dogwood, black cherry and hemlock. At 1.0 mile (1.6 km) turn left on Loop Trail where the Meadow Trail goes ahead, and at 1.2

miles (1.9 km) you again go left on the Loop Trail where the Polypody Trail goes right. Finally at 1.6 miles (2.5 km) you bear left on the Loop Trail where the Indian Pipe Trail goes right. Next you pass among some large boulders, and then you reach Inspiration Point. Here you get a view across Watson Run from the brink of a cliff. There is no guard rail, so be careful. Inspiration Point makes a good lunch stop.

Turn north through the hemlocks at the edge of the cliff. At 1.8 miles (2.9 km) turn left and descend to the Ravine Trail on which you turn right. (The Ravine Trail shares the narrow stream bottom with Watson Run. So at times of high water, you would do better to stick to the Loop Trail.) You soon cross Watson Run as best you can, and at 2.0 miles (3.2 km) there is an old mill site to the right of the trail. The mill was located at the confluence of Watson and Hesselgesser runs. All that remains is part of the stone dam on the far side, but this is certainly one of the gems of

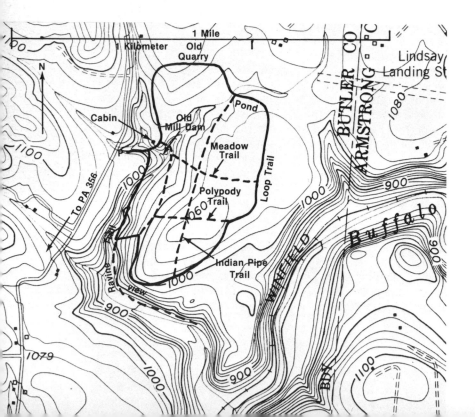

Goldenrod

Todd Sanctuary. Back on the trail, McCray Crossing is just around the bend. From here you retrace your steps to the parking lot or drop in at the cabin again.

The only other hike of any length descends Watson Run on the Ravine Trail to the edge of the Todd property. The private land beyond is closed to hikers, so you must retrace your steps.

34

Jennings Nature Reserve

Distance: 2.2 miles (3.5 km)
Time: 1½ hours
Rise: 240 feet (75 meters)
Highlights: Prairie wildflowers, massasauga
   rattlesnakes
Maps: USGS 7½' Slippery Rock; park map

Although most of Pennsylvania was heavily wooded at the time of settlement, there were a few bits of prairie. Here, on the beach of glacial Lake Edmund, was one of them. Found here are plants of western prairies, particularly the blazing star, which blooms in late July and early August and is worth a special trip. Many other wildflowers, including woodland types, also occur in the Reserve. So a visit any time from early spring to fall will likely find something in bloom. In all, 366 species of plants have been observed at Jennings.

The occurrence of the blazing star on a tract of only three acres was recognized by Dr. Otto E. Jennings, a botanist and educator. Dr. Jennings succeeded in getting the Western Pennsylvania Conservancy to purchase this 310-acre tract containing the tiny relict prairie. By clearing portions of the adjacent woodland, the prairie has since been expanded to about 20 acres. The bulk of the Reserve remains wooded. Subsequently, the Western Pennsylvania Conservancy transferred the Reserve to public ownership, and it is now operated by the Bureau of State Parks as an environmental education center.

The Reserve is also home to about a dozen massasauga rattlesnakes. The massasauga is shorter than the timber rattlesnake and prefers to live in swamps but is similarly shy and retiring. Stay on the established trails so you won't meet the massasauga unexpectedly. Should you be lucky enough to spot this elusive reptile, observe it from a distance with binoculars or telephoto lens.

The Jennings Reserve is located at the junction of PA 8, PA 173 and PA 528, about twelve miles north of Butler, four miles south of Slippery Rock, and three and one half miles from Moraine State Park. Leave your car on the north side of PA 528 adjacent to the prairie. The trails at Jennings are very muddy in wet weather, so good walking shoes or even hiking boots are advisable.

To start the hike, walk between the pillars marking the entrance to the Blazing Star Trail. Note the flowing or artesian well to the right of these pillars. After only 65 yards of this graveled path, you enter the prairie at the junction of the Massasauga Trail, on which you will return at the end of your hike. Look here for the blazing star. Note the evidence of man-made fire required to keep the forest from returning. Shortly, you pass on your right the Prairie Loop Trail, which you could take to lengthen your stay in the prairie. At the far side of the prairie bear right on the Deer Trail. At this point the trail junctions are all signed. At 0.4 mile (0.6 km) bear right on the Oakwoods Trail (White Oak Trail on park map). Shortly bear left, avoiding the maintenance trail that leads out to PA 173.

You will pass several old pits to the left of the trail. There seems to be some confusion as to what was mined

from these pits. The park map refers to them as ore (probably iron) pits, but local authorities claim limestone was quarried for the local charcoal iron furnaces. To the right of the trail three rows of daffodils give evidence of a vanished homestead.

At 0.8 mile (1.4 km) the trail follows an old fence marking the boundary of private land. Shagbark hickory and white oak are frequent trees along this section. Next, the trail follows along a small stream before crossing it without benefit of bridge.

Just after rounding a corner of private land, the unsigned White Oak alternate trail diverges to the left. Continue along the fence and descend into

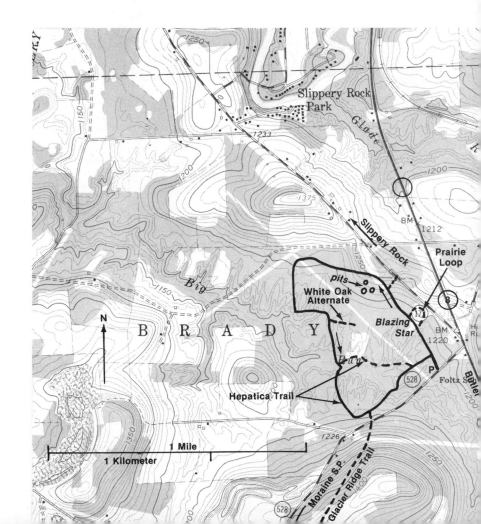

Drinking from an artesian well

the bottoms bordering Big Run. At 1.5 miles (2.4 km), you bear right on Hepatica Trail and shortly cross Big Run on a bridge. This bridge was in poor shape on my visit; if it is not passable, the Hepatica Trail in the opposite direction will lead you back to the shelter near the parking area.

Beyond Big Run the Hepatica Trail turns sharply left and climbs up the stream bank. It then passes an obscure junction with the Glacier Ridge Trail which proceeds southwest to Moraine State Park. The Glacier Ridge Trail is being rebuilt, and may be in much better shape at the time of your visit.

Continue on the Hepatica Trail passing through an old split rail fence. At 1.9 miles (3.0 km) you recross Big Run but this time on stepping stones. After climbing the stream bank you bear right on the Massasauga Trail, which soon passes the shelter and continues along the edge of the prairie to a junction with the Blazing Star Trail. Turn right here and it is just a few steps back to the parking lot.

There are further opportunities for walking in the Jennings Nature Reserve. This hike has bypassed a number of trails that can be used either to truncate it or extend it considerably. There are also trails to the south of PA 528 that visit the ruins of Foltz Mill. Just across PA 8 is the "Old Stone House", a replica of an inn dating from the 1820's. Guests were required to remove their boots in bed but were promised that there would be no more than five people per bed. The Old Stone House may have a new incarnation as a hostel for cyclists and hikers, if plans of the Pittsburgh Council of the American Youth Hostels are carried out.

35

Beechwood Nature Trails

Distance: 2.3 miles (3.7 km)
Time: 1¾ hours
Rise: 380 feet (115 meters)
Highlight: A pleasant walk
Maps: USGS 7½' Glenshaw; Nature Trail map
   (available at Evans Nature Center)

Beechwood Farms is a small nature reserve, within the Pittsburgh metropolitan area, owned by the Western Pennsylvania Conservancy and operated by the Western Pennsylvania Audubon Society. Because of its many steep-walled valleys, Pittsburgh has an abundance of undeveloped land, which frequently serves as a refuge for wildlife. Beechwood, a tract of upland once operated as a dairy farm, is being permitted to return to its natural state.

To reach Beechwood Farms, follow the directions to Hartwood Park (Hike 40) as far as the four-way stop on the green belt at Saxonburg Boulevard. Stay on Harts Run Road for 0.8 mile and then turn right on the Dorseyville Road at the stop sign. Another 0.3 mile brings you to the Beechwood parking lot, just across from the Fox Chapel fire department. Walking shoes are fine for this short hike. Don't forget your binoculars for a little birding.

While poison ivy grows on many trails in western Pennsylvania, at Beechwood it flourishes. If you're careful to stay on the well-cleared trails, you should be able to avoid contact with this weed. If you are unusually sensitive to poison ivy, probably you should wait until after several hard frosts have withered the leaves before you attempt the Beechwood Nature Trails. Poison ivy is an attractive and decorative vine. The settlers at Jamestown used it as a house plant, until they figured out what was making them itch.

Dogs are prohibited on the trails at Beechwood. Leave Rover at home so you won't have to lock him in your car. If the Evans Nature Center is open, visitors should register. There are plenty of exhibits, and you can go down the stairs to the basement where the restrooms are found and then use the back door to reach the trails. If the nature center is closed, wriggle through the wood fence. In either case, bear right and follow the sign to the Oak Forest Trail. All the trails are yellow-blazed, but only in wooded sections. The Oak Forest Trail descends the rise with a view of the farm pond, crosses a gravel road, and shortly reaches the first oaks along an old field boundary. You continue through the woods which also contain dogwood. This trail makes

Poison Ivy

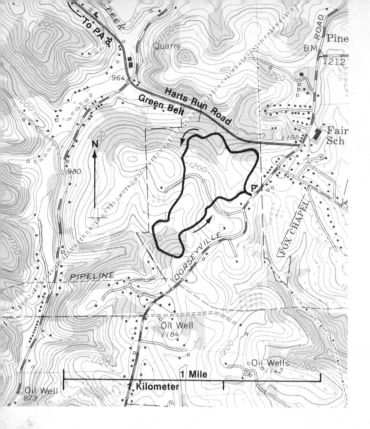

a close approach to Harts Run Road, which you can see through the trees even with the leaves on.

At 0.3 mile (0.5 km) you turn right on the Spring Hollow Trail. Continue the descent next to an old eroded road. You cross Harts Run at 0.4 mile (0.7 km) and then start the climb back to the uplands. There is a bench along the way with a possible leaves-off view. At the top of the hill you enter an old field, and at 0.8 mile (1.3 km) turn right on the Meadow View Trail. The Upper Fields Trail returns to the nature center. Here you pass a small stand of Hercules club and then cross a private driveway. Beyond the drive, you emerge into a field of poison ivy, and at 1.1 miles (1.7 km) you bear right on Pine Hollow Trail. You soon enter the woods and cross Beechwood Run on what was an old driveway. You climb the far side

of this valley through an old evergreen plantation. Red pines are encountered first, then white pines and finally larch. Next you cross an old road and, at 2.1 miles (3.3 km) bear right on the Meadow View Trail.

You pass a number of mulberry trees, always a favorite of fruit-eating birds. Shortly you turn left for the Meadow View Lookout, only 120 feet down the side trail, which provides a view across the meadows.

Back on the Meadow View Trail, you cross the private drive and then turn right on the Upper Fields Trail. Soon you are back at the Evans Nature Center and your car.

There are four cutoff trails, which could be used to shorten this hike, but no real opportunities for lengthening it. More trails are available at nearby Hartwood Park. (See Hike 40)

Harrison Hills Park

In-and-out distance: 2.3 miles (3.8 km)
Time: 1½ hours
Rise: 380 feet (115 m)
Highlights: Views, Rachel Carson Trail
Maps: USGS 7½' Freeport; Rachel Carson Trail
　　maps (available from American Youth Hostels
　　Pittsburgh Council)

Harrison Hills Park is in the extreme northeast corner of Allegheny County on the bluffs above the Allegheny River. In 1949 members of the newly-formed Pittsburgh Council of the American Youth Hostels were on a canoe trip. The cliffs inspired them to build a cross-country foot trail from Pittsburgh to Cook Forest State Park. The trail was named after Horace Forbes Baker, who established the Pittsburgh Council shortly before his death. Originally, the Baker Trail started at the Highland Park bridge over the Allegheny. Rapid development soon forced abandonment of all 25 miles of the trail in Allegheny County. (See also Hike 41.)

An attempt was made in the early seventies to salvage parts of the original Baker Trail and weld them into a new trail across northern Allegheny County. This trail passes close to the birthplace of Rachel Carson, the environmentalist. Rachel Carson is known best for her books, *The Sea Around Us* (1951) and *Silent Spring* (1962). The latter warned of the dangers of herbicides and pesticides, particularly DDT.

A 33-mile trail was finally blazed, stretching from North Park to Harrison Hills, mostly on private land. This hike takes you along one of the few sections on public land. It is also part of the original Baker Trail.

Harrison Hills Park can be reached only from old PA 28. It is on the east side of the highway, north of Birdville and about half a mile beyond the traffic lights at the GeeBee shopping center. Just inside the park entrance take the left fork of the road and follow it to its end in a parking lot (one of several near the cliffs), about 0.9 mile from the highway. Drinking water and restrooms are available at the picnic area. There is some poison ivy along the trail, and the cliffs are unforgiving. Keep a tight hold on children and dogs. Walking shoes are fine despite some wet places.

From the parking lot, head across the open area past the picnic shelter to a break in the trees that provides a view across the Allegheny into Westmoreland County. Then turn left and pick up the yellow blazes of the Rachel Carson Trail where it heads into the woods. The trail pops back into the picnic area again before committing itself to the woods.

Generally the path you want is the one closest to the edge of the cliffs. The blazes are too infrequent to be of much help. Beware of some unmarked trails, which are reputed to descend steeply all the way to the river. At 0.4 mile (0.7 km) you cross a stream, which you can hear cascading over the cliff. There is a view to the right of the trail at the brink of the cliff. Soon a mowed path comes in from the left, and you should bear right on it.

Shortly, another side stream is encountered. Take the first path leaving the mowed path, cross the stream and continue along the edge. At 0.8 mile (1.3 km) there is a view of the PA 356 bridge at Freeport. Basswood trees and service berries grow right at the brink. Next, you descend and continue north below the edge of the bluffs. Cross a stream in a deep ravine at 0.9 mile (1.5 km) and then climb back to the top of the hill. Finally, bear right through the woods to a metal-walled spring at 1.2 miles (1.9 km). Beyond this point the trail seems to vanish. Actually, it ends at old PA 28. Turn and retrace your steps to your car.

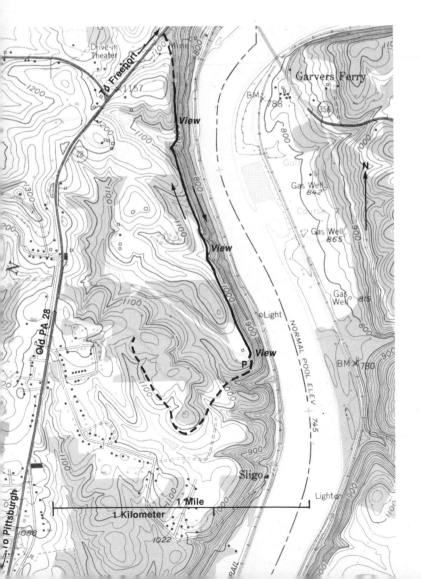

View of Allegheny River

37

Raccoon Creek Wildflower Reserve

Distance: 2.4 miles (3.9 km)
Time: 1½ hours
Rise: 100 feet (30 meters)
Highlight: Wildflowers
Maps: USGS 7½' Aliquippa, Clinton; state
   park map

Raccoon Creek State Park is located in Beaver County about 25 miles west of Pittsburgh. It is a large park by Pennsylvania standards and was established by the National Park Service back in the Great Depression through the acquisition of submarginal farm land. Ruins of some of these farms can still be found in the undeveloped western portions of the park. Despite its name, most of the park occupies the valley of Traverse Creek. This hike is in the only part of the park on Raccoon Creek. This is the small portion east of US 30, set aside as a wildflower reserve and originally purchased by the Western Pennsylvania Conservancy. It was transferred to the state in 1971.

The only entrance to the wildflower reserve is from US 30, about 3 miles west of Clinton. Pets are not permitted on the trails of the wildflower reserve. So do your pet a favor and don't bring it. Then you won't have to leave it in your car while you hike. Drive through the evergreen plantation and park. If time permits—and this is a short easy hike—stop in at the nature center. The trails might be a little muddy but ordinary walking shoes should be fine.

The best time to visit Raccoon Creek for spring wildflowers is the second week of May.

The hike starts on the Jennings Trail at the far end of the parking area. The Jennings Trail has the greatest variety of plant life, and it also intersects many other trails, permitting you to vary or truncate the hike. Moving along the Jennings Trail, you climb a small hill and then circle around Hungerford Cabin. Hungerford was a cartoonist for the *Pittsburgh Press and Post Gazette,* and this cabin was his second home. Second homes were modest in those days. Beyond the clearing, use the switchbacks to descend the slope. At 0.3 mile (0.4 km) the Deer Trail goes left and shortly the Big Maple Trail does the same. Along this section you can see woodland wildflowers such as May apples and hepatica. These wildflowers must grow and bloom in the few short weeks of spring before the deciduous trees leaf out. At 0.4 mile (0.6 km) the trail crosses a small stream and at 0.5 mile (0.8 km) it reaches the top of a low cliff. You can either bear right and descend the stone steps, which are in rather poor shape, or bear left and de-

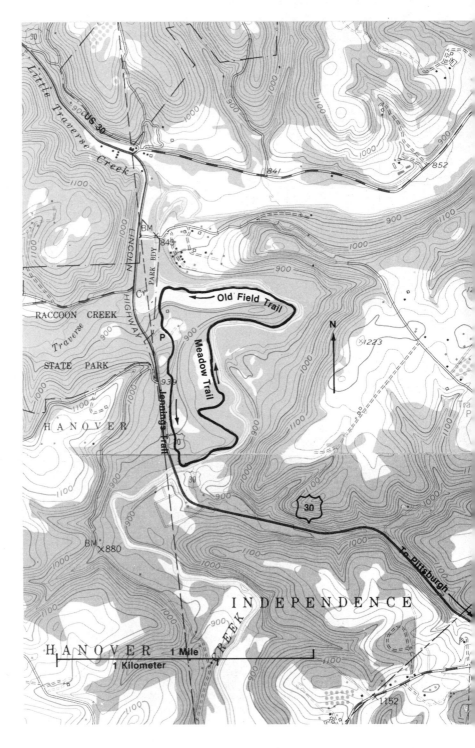

Jack-in-the-Pulpit

scend on a newer trail. You may notice some poison ivy along the trail.

In these bottom lands look for trillium and Virginia bluebell. Also note the wood duck box on a post in the slough. There are a great many bird boxes installed in the wildflower reserve. They are all worth a hard look, as they may have interesting tenants. Different species of trees grow here in the bottom land. Largest of these is the sycamore with its peeling light-colored bark. The silence on the bottom land is frequently broken by jets taking off from the Greater Pittsburgh Airport.

The Jennings Trail hugs the base of the upland and passes the Big Oak (now dead) shown on the park map. At 0.9 mile (1.4 km) you turn full right on the Old Wagon Road Trail, avoiding another trail that parallels the Jennings. The Old Wagon Road Trail takes you out onto the bottom land towards Raccoon Creek. At 1.0 mile (1.6 km) you bear left on the Meadow Trail and enter a large meadow on the bottom land. The open meadow is a very different environment. Here one may find wildflowers blooming in the summer and into the fall. Bird boxes may harbor the rare eastern bluebird.

At 1.3 miles (2.1 km) turn right on the Jennings Trail again, which lies between the base of the cliffs and Raccoon Creek. Note the large tulip trees growing on the bottom land.

At 1.6 miles (2.7 km) you turn right on the Old Field Trail at the junction with the Audubon Trail. This trail takes you back to the creek and then between the creek and the old field. Keep left at 1.7 miles (2.8 km) at an obscure trail junction. Ignore a cutoff trail and then bear right at a trail junction. Then circle back to a junction with the Henrici Trail at 2.3 miles (3.7 km). Henrici was an outdoor writer from Sewickly. Turn right and climb back up the hill. At the top, bear right on the road. The parking lot is visible ahead.

There are some other hiking opportunities in the western part of Raccoon State Park. The Nichol Road is gated off for most of its length and makes a pleasant walk through woods, meadows and fields. But the park map is inaccurate with respect to trails. The hiking trails shown southeast of Nichol Road are actually connected, but the Bridle Trail to the northwest has been abandoned and can only be followed near its ends.

McConnells Mill State Park

Distance: 3¼ miles (5.2 km)
Time: 2 hours
Rise: 340 feet (103 meters)
Highlights: Gorge, waterfalls, rapids,
   wildflowers, old mill, covered bridge
Maps: USGS 7½' Portersville; state park map

Geologically, the gorge of Slippery Rock Creek is quite recent, dating only from the last ice age. Before the ice age, Slippery Rock and Muddy creeks both flowed northwest to the St. Lawrence River. But with that way blocked by the continental ice sheet, large lakes formed in the valleys of the creeks. As the ice began to retreat, glacial Lake Arthur found a new outlet here, and the enormous flow of meltwater cut this gorge in only a few thousand years. Today, Slippery Rock Creek flows to the Ohio, and its gorge has become one of the few unspoiled hemlock ravines in the western part of the state. Twelve species of fern are found at McConnells Mill State Park, more than anywhere else in western Pennsylvania.

McConnells Mill State Park is about 40 miles north of Pittsburgh, just 0.3 mile west of the junction of US 422 with US 19 and 1.7 miles west of I-79. Turn south off US 422, and it is another 0.7 mile to the parking lot at the Johnson Road junction where this hike begins. In driving south from US 422, you cross two of the sites where glacial Lake Arthur drained into Slippery Rock Gorge.

Good walking shoes are adequate for this hike. This hike is best avoided in winter, as seep springs coat the rocks with ice and footing becomes extremely treacherous. The spring wild flowers are usually at their peak around the third week in May.

To start your hike, walk north along the road about 100 yards to the Alpha Pass trailhead. A small stream flows over the edge of the Homewood Sandstone here, creating a small waterfall. This is one of the sites where glacial Lake Arthur drained its torrent into the gorge. At that time the ground here would have shaken under your feet. Head down the steep but short Alpha Pass Trail and reach the trail along the creek in another 100 yards. This trail is marked with yellow paint blazes of irregular size and shape. There are several opportunities here to view the rapids in Slippery Rock Creek from the large blocks of sandstone that have slid down the side of the gorge.

Turn left and head downstream on this rough trail. At 0.3 mile (0.5 km) you pass a junction with the trail you will use at the end of your hike. Continue downstream on smoother trail. Note the sizeable hemlocks that grow in the gorge. The evergreen shrub growing on some of the boulders is American yew. At 0.6 mile (1.0 km) you arrive at McConnells Mill. In the nineteenth century this wild and rugged location was of value not for its beauty but for its energy. When Thomas McConnell modernized his newly purchased mill in 1875, water power was still holding its own against steam. The mill is still in operating order and on occasion is opened to the public. The mill and adjacent property were obtained by the Western Pennsylvania Conservancy and later conveyed to the state. Just beyond the mill is a covered bridge dating from 1874. You will return across this bridge, so pass it by for now and continue on the self-guiding Kildoo Nature Trail. The Kildoo Trail is paved! Enjoy it while you

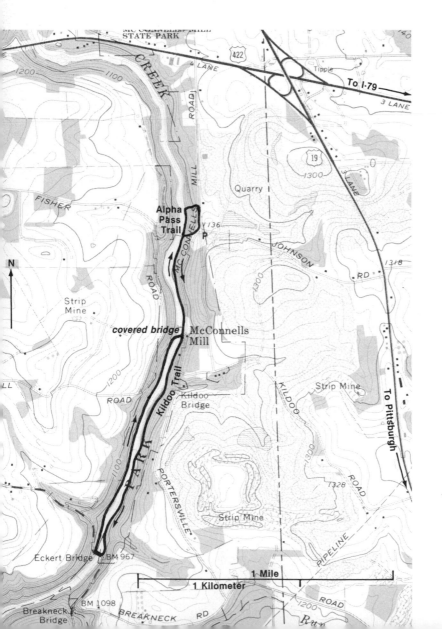

Covered Bridge

can, for there is plenty of rough trail ahead with rocks and mud.

McConnells was not the only mill to use Slippery Rock Creek. At post 7 look for the ruins of another mill. At 0.9 mile (1.4 km) you cross a footbridge over Kildoo Creek. Here you leave the paved trail behind and continue on rough trail. Keep watch just beyond here for millstones from an abandoned grist mill.

You reach the Eckert Bridge at 1.7 miles (2.7 km). Cross this bridge and turn right at the far side on the return trail. Note the millstone mounted on a pedestal just beyond the bridge. By far the largest part of McConnells Mill State Park lies downstream from the Eckert Bridge. Fishermen have worn trails starting here, but it is at least 3.5 miles to the Harris Bridge, the next one downstream, and most of this distance is probably devoid of trail. Still there is a real opportunity for the adventurous hiker to explore the deeper portions of Slippery Rock Gorge.

Moving upstream you pass repeated displays of white and red trillium in season. Elsewhere trillium is rare. But when conditions are right, they may be abundant. This trail is much less used than the Kildoo and you may well experience moments when you seem to be alone in the gorge.

At 2.7 miles (4.3 km) you turn right and wait your chance to cross the covered bridge. Auto traffic is one way at a time on the bridge, and you may have to take the bridge on the run when the traffic changes direction. This brings you back to the mill for one last look and a drink at the fountain.

If the traffic is very light, follow the road back to the parking lot. It is an easy climb and passes between house-sized blocks of sandstone. If traffic is at its usual heavy level, head upstream along the trail and at 3.1 miles (5.0 km) turn right at the sign to the parking lot. The climb is steep but short, and you are soon back to your car.

Other attractions in McConnells Mill State Park are Cleland Rock and Hells Hollow Trail. Cleland Rock provides views of Slippery Rock Gorge and is reached from Breakneck Bridge Road. Hells Hollow Trail leads to a waterfall and an old iron furnace and is located on the west side of the park.

Yellow Creek State Park

Distance: 3.2 miles (5.2 km)
Time: 2 hours
Rise: 200 feet (60 m)
Highlight: Yellow Creek Lake
Maps: USGS 7½' Brush Valley; state park map

Yellow Creek State Park is located on the old Kittaning Indian Path (now US 422) in Indiana County. The park was created as part of a state park expansion program in the sixties and seventies. An earth-and-rock dam just north of Moose Hill on Yellow Creek converted about one-fourth of the land into a lake. Three hiking trails have been built. This hike uses the longest trail in the most remote corner of the park.

Although the trailhead can be reached by paved road, persistence is required. From US 422 turn past the park office on PA 259 and continue past the turnoff for the beach area. PA 259 then leaves the park, but you should keep going and take the first paved road to the right after Campground Road. It is another 2.2 miles, past Gramma's Cove, to the parking area at the end of the road, which is the start of the Damsite Trail. This road had no identification at the time of my visit. If you miss this critical turn, you will reach Brush Valley in 1.2 miles. To reach the trailhead from US 119, turn east on PA 56 at Homer City. After 5.4 miles, turn left on PA 259 in Brush Valley. Then in 1.2 miles turn left onto the unsigned road.

As I put on my boots and got my pack and measuring wheel out of the car I heard a loud humming. At first I thought I had parked next to a dead animal. But then I saw a vague cloud approaching across the meadow. As I watched, the cloud moved out into the parking area, and I could see some of the individual insects. It was a swarm o' wild honeybees following a new queen to a new hive. Honeybees were introduced to North America by the colonists. To the Indians honeybees were the white man's flies. Their arrival, about 200 miles ahead of the frontier, was bad news for the native Americans. As I watched from a respectful distance, the swarm began to cluster on a small tree. I set off down the trail.

The first section of the trail is a mowed path through a meadow paralleling the edge of a pine plantation. The path doubles once to avoid a wet spot. At 0.4 mile (0.7 km) the trail enters the woods and then swings left, avoiding another trail that goes straight down the hillside. There are some orange paint blazes in the woods. Black cherry trees

Swarm of Bees

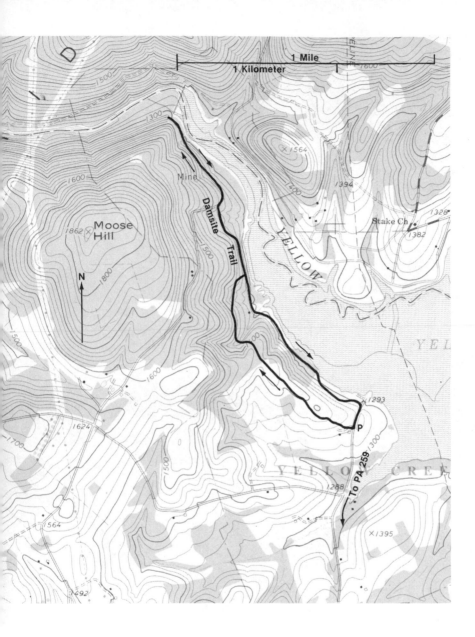

grow along this section. Soon you pass
a bench that might provide a leaves-off
view of the lake. Then you cross a
stream on a log bridge and continue
across a concrete foundation. You
cross another stream at 0.7 mile (1.2

km) on the slippery remains of a low
bridge and then pass through a closely-
spaced cluster of service berries.

At 0.8 mile (1.3 km) you meet the old
road near the lake shore and turn left
toward the dam. There are some sizable

trees along this section, and the lake is visible between them. At 1.2 miles (1.9 km) you bear right on a jeep road down the hillside and soon pass two pairs of gateposts—one of wood and one of steel. At 1.6 miles (2.6 km) you reach the edge of the dam above the spillway.

To return, retrace your steps, being sure to bear left just after the wooden gateposts. To vary the return route, continue ahead along the old road at 2.4 miles (3.9 km). There is some poison ivy along the edge of the road, but you shouldn't have any trouble keeping out of it. Soon there is a view of the lake, but better ones lie ahead.

Your route takes you along the lower edge of the pine plantation. The old road dips under the lake, so bear right on the bulldozed replacement, which provides good views across the lake. At 3.1 miles (5.0 km) you turn right on the paved road, shortly after it emerges from the lake. Climb the rise and you are back at the trailhead.

Hartwood Park

Distance: 3.5 miles (5.7 km)
Time: 2¼ hours
Rise: 300 feet (90 meters)
Highlights: Mansion, deer
Maps: USGS 7½' Glenshaw; park maps*

Hartwood Park is a 629-acre estate in Allegheny County that once belonged to John and Mary Flinn Lawrence. The Lawrence mansion is open for tours, but only by appointment. The park is also a center for the performing arts. Concerts are given and plays performed on a large outdoor stage at the edge of a field towards the western end of the park. The Lawrences were devoted to horseback riding. They provided their estate with a stable, which is still in use, but not open to the public, and a network of bridle trails. In the winter, these trails attract cross-country skiers, but they are available to hikers the rest of the year. In the heavily-wooded parts of the park it is hard to believe you are in the second largest metropolitan area in the state.

The parking area at Hartwood can be reached only from Saxonburg Boulevard. From exit 4 on the Pennsylvania Turnpike, go south on PA 8 for 3.0 miles and then turn left on the Greenbelt, which at this point is Harts Run Road.

The Greenbelt is one of several

systems of roads that encircle Pittsburgh. Follow the Greenbelt for 2.9 miles to a four-way stop. Here you turn left on Saxonburg Boulevard for 1.1 miles to the park entrance. It is another 0.5 mile to the parking lot near the mansion where this hike begins. Owing to the horses, there is a lot of muddy trail on this hike, so boots are indicated. It can be done with ordinary walking shoes, if you don't mind getting a bit wet. Dogs are permitted on the trails but must be kept on leash. Restrooms are available on the far side of the mansion in the old garage.

To start the hike, walk to the parking lot entrance and turn right on the paved road. At the fork in the road bear left toward the stable and at the next bend continue straight ahead on the lower Lawrence Loop. The park trails are not signed, and the three park maps I obtained all differed substantially with respect to the location and names of trails. But the park isn't large, so you can't possibly stay lost for long. You will soon run into one of the primary trails or a park boundary.

At 0.3 mile (0.4 km) you pass the Oak

*Available from Allegheny County Parks, Penn-Liberty Plaza, 1520 Penn Avenue, Pittsburgh, PA 15222.

Hartwood

Trail on your right, and at 0.5 mile (0.8 km) the Connecting Trail comes in from the right. To the left you can see a field and barn for the resident horses. Turn left at 0.9 mile (1.5 km) on the upper Lawrence Loop, cross a pipe line and shortly pass an unnamed trail on your left. Then bear left at the edge of an extensive field. To your right is the large open air stage mentioned earlier.

Follow the road out to the edge of Middle Road and turn right along the fence. At 1.6 miles (2.6 km) you pass through an old orchard and then turn right on the Middle Road Trail. Back at the east edge of the field you cross a stream and then turn left around the edge of Flinn Fields. At 2.0 miles (3.2 km) a trail goes left into the woods. Keep a sharp lookout for deer, who like to feed in this field and shelter in the surrounding woods. At the far edge of the field, the trail enters a stand of white pine and then turns right on the pipe line. Cross Little Pine Creek as

best you can and continue along the edge of the field. At 2.3 miles (3.7 km) you reenter the woods and immediately turn left on the North Trail. Soon you pass the Pump House Trail on your right, then an unnamed trail, and at 2.9 miles (4.7 km) you reach the five corners. Here you jog right and continue on the least-used trail. This is the Hunters Trail, and you follow it across a stream to a junction with the Saxonburg and Pine trails at 3.3 miles (5.2 km). Turn right, uphill, on the Pine Trail and climb to the pine plantation, which gives this trail its name. Keep a lookout for poison ivy, which occurs here along with Virginia creeper. Continue across a ravine on the Pine Trail and cut right across a field to the parking lot and your car.

Many other trails thread the southern part of Hartwood, and if they aren't too muddy, they provide additional hiking opportunities. Also, Beechwood Nature Trails are nearby. (See Hike 35.)

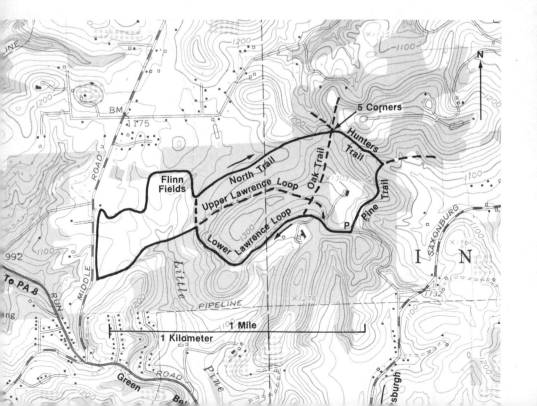

41

Crooked Creek State Park

In-and-out distance: 4.0 miles (6.5 km)
Time: 2 hours
Rise: 100 feet (30 m)
Highlight: Baker Trail
Maps: USGS 7½' Whitesburg; state park map;
    Baker Trail Guide, map 4

Crooked Creek State Park is centered on a flood control reservoir built by the Army Corps of Engineers in 1940 in Armstrong County, northeast of Pittsburgh. This hike follows one of the few sections of the Baker Trail on public land.

The Baker Trail was built by the Pittsburgh Council of American Youth Hostels, starting in 1949, and was named for the founder of the Pittsburgh Council, Horace Forbes Baker. Built largely on private land, the trail originally ran from the north end of Highland Park Bridge in Pittsburgh to Cook Forest State Park, about 125 miles to the northeast. In those days a farmer would gladly permit a hiking trail to pass through his wood lot, along the edge of a field and past the barn, because it guaranteed him people to talk with. Nowadays the farm has become an industrial park or been cut up into second home sites, so the trail is severed or rerouted on roads, most of them paved. Thus all the Baker Trail in Allegheny County has been lost, and the southern end has retreated northward to Schenley.

Crooked Creek State Park is the closest to Pittsburgh that the Baker Trail crosses public land. In this hike the trail follows and crosses Cherry Run, a tributary of Crooked Creek in the eastern part of the park. Since Crooked Creek is a flood control reservoir, the trail may be under water, briefly, in spring.

The trailhead is on PA 359, just east of the bridge over Crooked Creek, about 6 miles north of PA 56 at Spring Church and 12 miles south of US 422 at Kittanning. There is an ample pulloff on the south side of the road. Several wooden signs identify the Baker Trail crossing. The hike follows an old road along Cherry Run. So walking shoes should be enough, except for the crossing of Cherry Run near the end of the hike, where boots would be useful. This is described as an in-and-out hike. But as the far end on the Cherry Run Road can be reached by car, a shuttle is possible. There is some poison ivy in the bottom lands, but it does not encroach on the trail. The best time for this hike is in the spring, after the high water and when the wild flowers are in bloom but before

Skunk Cabbage

the trees leaf out.

To start the hike, dodge around the steel gate and follow the yellow-blazed old road down to the bottom lands. Trees along here include sycamore, walnut, chokecherry, basswood, elm, hickory and apple. You may notice an occasional sting of nettles, but they aren't really a problem. At 0.4 mile (0.6 km) you pass a wet weather waterfall that comes down over the cliffs to the left, and soon you may also pass a bee tree containing an active hive. At several places you cross stream beds that come down through breaks in the hillside to the left. At 0.9 mile (1.4 km) there is a view of Cherry Run, but mostly the run bends away to the far side of the valley. It appears to be named for the chokecherry, not the black cherry. At 1.4 miles (2.3 km) an old road comes in from the left, and immediately beyond, you reach the crossing of Cherry Run.

Just upstream at the abutment of an old road bridge, the American Youth Hostels built a cable bridge across Cherry Run. It consisted of two steel cables, one about five feet above the other, attached to trees on either side

of the river. Motorcycles and snowmobiles can't cross a cable bridge. As for the hiker, he puts his feet on the lower wire and holds onto the upper one. Then he sidesteps across the stream. Too much tension on the cables can uproot one of the trees; if there is too much slack, the hiker may suddenly find himself attempting handstands as the cables invert. Relax. The tree on the far side has fallen down, making this bridge uncrossable. You must either ford the run, or cross on stepping stones found a little downstream.

Beyond Cherry Run, the trail swings through a meadow and climbs a high bank through a dense, dark stand of hemlocks. You pass the entrance to a field on the right and then drop down to cross a small stream at 1.9 miles (3.1 km).

Continue around the bend to a steel gate at the edge of Cherry Run Road. The Baker Trail turns right and follows the road uphill. To return to your car, retrace your steps along the bottom lands of Cherry Run. Other hiking opportunities are found on the Shore Line and Laurel Point trails in the west end of the park, near the campground.

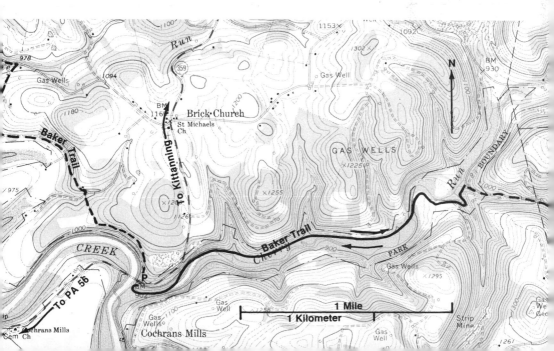

Moraine State Park

Distance: 4.5 miles (7.2 km)
Time: 2.6 hours
Rise: 1,050 feet (320 meters)
Highlights: Glacier Ridge Trail, Lake Arthur
Maps: USGS 7½' Prospect; state park map

Moraine State Park is located about one hour north of Pittsburgh at the junction of I-79 and US 422. Glacial lakes Arthur and Edmond, just to the north, were created when the continental glacier blocked the valleys of Slippery Rock and Muddy creeks. A dam on Muddy Creek recreates Lake Arthur, although the original lake was considerably higher and some six miles longer. The terminal moraines of the Illinoian Ice Sheet and two major advances of the Wisconsin glacier are located just to the north and west of Moraine State Park. Before the park could be opened to the public, over 400 abandoned oil, gas and water wells had to be plugged to stop seepage that would have polluted the lake.

Most recreational opportunities at Moraine utilize Lake Arthur, but the roadless northern shore has an attraction for hikers in a section of the Glacier Ridge Trail. The modest section of the Glacier Ridge Trail currently in existence is scheduled for extension in both directions. To the northeast it will be extended entirely on public land to the Old Stone House on PA 8. To the west it will be extended across private land to McConnells Mill State Park on Slippery Rock Creek. But these extensions are only a beginning. Plans also call for the incorporation of the Glacier Ridge Trail into Pennsylvania's portion of the 3,200 mile North Country Trail, which is to extend from Crown Point in New York to the Missouri River in North Dakota.

This hike is described here using a car shuttle. If only one car is available, the hike could be done as an "in-and-out hike", doubling the length. Use of the side trail loops to Davis Hollow Marina and the PA 528 bridge to vary the return route would increase the length to the "boot buster" category. The main Glacier Ridge Trail in the park is blue-blazed while side trails are yellow-blazed. Ordinary walking shoes should be adequate.

The car shuttle is lengthy and complicated, so pay careful attention and keep an eye on the odometer. From I-79 turn east on PA 488, and then in about 1 mile turn north on Pleasant Valley Road. After entering the park, turn west on US 422, cross an arm of Lake Arthur, and then exit right onto North Shore Drive. Continue on North

Beaver-felled Trees

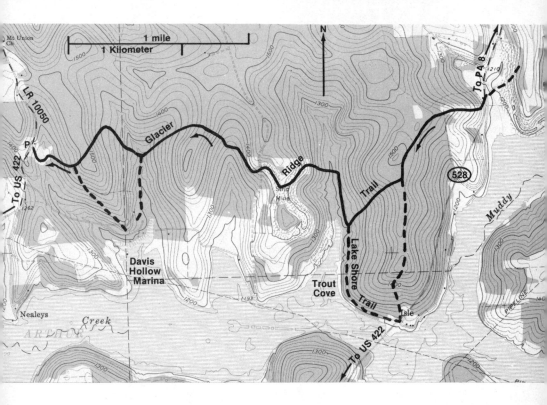

Shore Drive past Lakeview day use area and Watts Bay Marina to the stop sign at the access road to the Davis Hollow Marina. Turn left here on LR (Legislative Route) 10050, and it is just 0.3 mile north to Glacier Ridge trailhead. There is enough parking space here for two or three cars. Leave one car and continue north. In 1.1 miles turn right at the intersection with Reichert Road. This is still LR 10050, and you will stay on it until a T junction at 3.0 miles from the Glacier Ridge trailhead. Across the field ahead and to the left at this junction is a beautiful example of an esker, once the bed of a meltwater stream flowing under the continental glacier but now a low hill. Turn right at this junction with LR 10065 and follow it to the crossroads of West Liberty at 4.9 miles. Next, turn right on the West Liberty

Road. Just south of West Liberty, turn left and shortly bear right at successive junctions coming to PA 528 at 7.1 miles. Turn right on PA 528 to the Glacier Ridge Trail crossing at a total distance of 8.2 miles. Park along the highway across from the access road to a boat launch area. There are several temptations along this car shuttle to attempt shortcuts, but they probably won't save any time and should be resisted.

At last you are ready to start the Glacier Ridge Trail. Cross under the power line and climb left up the hillside. After 200 yards the trail skirts a corner of private land and turns away from the power line. Continue climbing through a grove of dogwood to reach the top of the hill at 0.4 mile (0.7 km). At 0.8 mile (1.2 km) you pass under another power line. Note the occurrence of hercules club along this swath. It is a straight-trunked shrub with doubly compound leaves and sharp thorns. Shortly beyond the swath, bear right where the yellow-blazed side trail continues ahead to the PA 528 bridge. Follow the Glacier Ridge Trail down to the edge of Trout Cove where you turn right. To the left, the yellow-blazed Lake Shore Trail also goes to the PA 528 bridge, offering a possible side loop. As you move along the Glacier Ridge Trail, note the evidence of beaver in felled aspen trees near the water's edge.

At 1.6 miles (2.7 km) you cross a bridge over a stream and start to climb the next ridge. At the top of the hill you enter a meadow, which is actually a reclaimed strip mine. Part way across, bear right on a jeep road paralleling a white pine plantation. At the far edge of the old mine cross a dirt road, reenter the woods, and descend. The point at which the trail reenters the woods is obscure, so pay close attention. At 2.4 miles (3.8 km) turn right on a woods road and then cross a stream on stepping stones. Next you climb over a third ridge to a trail junction in the next valley at 3.4 miles (5.4 km), just after another stream crossing on rocks. To the left, a yellow-blazed trail leads to the Davis Hollow Marina. You turn right on the blue-blazed Glacier Ridge Trail and soon cross another stream. At 3.8 miles (6.1 km) turn sharply left off the old woods road and continue climbing to the top of the ridge. Another yellow-blazed trail from the Davis Hollow Marina comes in at 4.2 miles (6.8 km), providing a second loop for varying the route back, if you didn't arrange a car shuttle. After crossing another stream and passing through a row of arbor vitae, turn left and skirt the edge of a small pond. There must have been a house here before the park was formed. Beyond the pond you climb briefly through an evergreen plantation to LR 10050 where you dropped off your other car.

Other hiking opportunities are available at Jennings Nature Reserve, about four miles up PA 528 at the junction with PA 8. (See Hike 34). McConnells Mills State Park is just a couple of miles west of I-79, and a hike there (Hike 38) is also described in this book.

Ryerson Station State Park

Distance: 5.3 miles (8.6 km)
Time: 3 hours
Rise: 800 feet (240 m)
Highlight: Ryerson Lake
Maps: USGS 7½' Wind Ridge; state park map

Ryerson Station State Park consists of only 1,164 acres on the north branch of the Dunkard Fork of Wheeling Creek, in Greene County, a few miles from the West Virginia line. It's named after Fort Ryerson, built nearby in 1792 by order of Virginia authorities. The fort was a place of refuge for settlers during Indian raids.

Ryerson Station State Park can be reached from PA 21 about 22 miles west of I-79 or from PA 18 about nine miles from Holbrook. From PA 21 turn east on LR (Legislative Route) 30039 for 0.8 mile and then turn right, crossing the ford below the Ryerson Lake dam. Continue for 0.7 mile to the large parking area that serves the picnic area and trailhead. Ordinary walking shoes are suitable for this hike.

To the right of the map board at the trailhead move into the woods on the Fox Feather Trail and shortly turn right on the Lazear Trail. The Lazear Trail, named after a former landowner, passes through some spruce plantings. At 0.3 mile (0.5 km) you pass a "wolf tree" to the right of the trail. This white oak, thought to be 300 years old, grew wide, spreading branches that now shade out trees underneath. Thus it

wolfs down the sunlight. This eliminates the competition but doesn't produce much saw timber. "Wolf tree" is an expression used by foresters.

Soon you also pass some poison ivy. Note the furry or hairy appearance of this well-established vine, which can help you to identify poison ivy even in winter.

At 0.5 mile (0.8 km) the Orchard Trail diverges left, but you bear right, passing a shagbark hickory. The top of the hill is reached at 0.8 mile (1.3 km) and provides a view of the lake more than 400 feet below. Continuing on the Lazear Trail, you pass through a small meadow with more poison ivy before the trail descends into Mennell Hollow. Along the way you pass a sycamore "wolf tree." The Tiffany Ridge Trail diverges to the left at 1.4 miles (2.3 km). The trails on this hill are liberally provided with benches, should you decide to sit down and rest or contemplate.

Shortly beyond the Tiffany Ridge Trail you pass a large white oak killed by lightning. The Tiffany Ridge Trail rejoins the Lazear Trail at 1.8 miles (2.8 km) as does the Fox Feather shortly beyond: At

Wolf Tree

WOLF TREE

OVER 300 YEARS AGO THIS OAK TREE
WAS THE ONLY TREE GROWING IN WHAT
WAS THEN AN OPEN AREA. IT RECEIVED
SUNLIGHT FROM ALL SIDES, SO IT GREW
IN ALL DIRECTIONS. NOW THAT THE WOODS
HAS GROWN UP AROUND IT, IT STILL
DOMINATES THE AREA BY CREATING SHADE
WHICH PREVENTS OTHER TREES FROM
GROWING UNDER IT. HENCE THE NAME
WOLF TREE

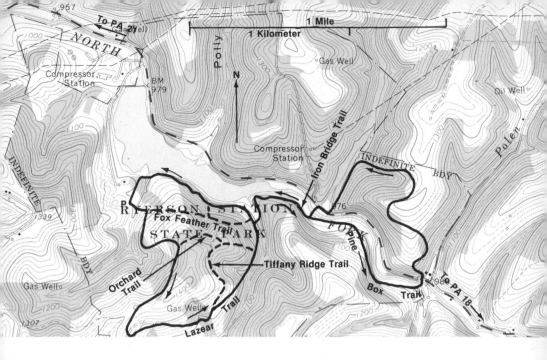

1.9 miles (3.1 km) you turn right on the Iron Bridge Trail, cross the stream in the bottom of the hollow and soon emerge along the edge of Ryerson Lake. Occasional bass croaks from the bottom of the bank announce the presence of bullfrogs. The Iron Bridge itself is reached at 2.3 miles (3.7 km). It once served a road across the North Fork but now carries only foot traffic. You will cross it on your way back, so pass it by for now and continue on the Pine Box Trail along the water's edge. Ignore a swath to the right, and at 2.7 miles (4.3 km) you climb the stream bank. Shortly after, you emerge into a field. At 2.9 miles (4.7 km) you turn left on the road and cross a bridge over the North Fork to reach L.R. 30039. Cross this paved road and bear left on the Pine Box Trail. Continue up the hill to 3.3 miles (5.3 km) where the trail leads ahead to the Stahl Cemetery. Now you see the origin of the Pine Box Trail. More than forty people came up this hill in pine boxes. Curiously, there aren't any Stahls in the Stahl Cemetery.

Mostly they were named Chess or Parson.

Back on the Pine Box Trail, you continue around the side of the hill along the contour before descending along the edge of a ravine that contains some large oaks. At the bottom of Applegate Hollow you bear left and reach L.R. 30039 at 4.3 miles (6.8 km). Turn right, cross the Iron Bridge, retrace your route on the Iron Bridge Trail and then turn right on the Lazear Trail. At 4.9 miles (7.8 km) there is a view of the lake. Keep right and you will come out at the edge of the lake. Cross a bridge next to the lake and follow the trail cut into the hillside. This brings you to a confusing four-way trail junction at 5.1 miles (8.1 km). Turn right to return to the lake shore. Pass behind the boat rental hut and bear left through the picnic area past a drinking fountain and restrooms to the parking lot.

There are other hikes in Ryerson Station State Park on the Three Mitten, Polly Hollow, Iron Bridge and Deer trails north of the lake.

Erie and the North

Pine Swamp Natural Area

Distance: 2.2 miles (3.5 km)
Time: 2 hours
Rise: 40 feet (12 m)
Highlights: High bush blueberry, spring wild flowers
Maps: USGS 7½' Sandy Lake; Western
    Pennsylvania Conservancy brochure

For the adventurous, Pine Swamp provides something unusual: a wetland hike. On a wetland hike you are going to get wet and muddy. So dress accordingly. Don't get your good hiking boots soaked; wear sneakers or some old shoes instead. Wear long pants, as the marsh grasses are razor edged and will slice you up if you wear shorts. Insect repellent, in quantity and strength, is also in order.

What could possibly lure hikers off dry ground to slosh through a bog, up to their knees if they don't lose their balance, or higher if they do? Well, Pine Swamp Natural Area is the lair of the high bush blueberry. When they ripen the last week of July, people wade right in to get them. Another good time to visit Pine Swamp is in late April or early May, before trees leaf out. Then the wild flowers will be in bloom, and the insect populations will still be low.

A change of clothes should be left in the car, together with a couple of liters of water for each person to rinse off with. The swamp has no landmarks. So you had better make sure your compass

Trail Junction in Pine Swamp Natural Area

is in your pack or pocket, in case you lose sight of the blazes. A compass permits you to keep going in a more-or-less straight line rather than in circles. At Pine Swamp, you would head south to return to the highway.

Pine Swamp is a northern bog and presumably started out as a shallow lake, after the retreat of the last ice sheet. The glacier confused the drainage. So this lake had two outlets, Wolf Creek to the south and Fox Run to the west. Gradually the lake filled in with peat, and trees began to grow. But parts of the swamp, such as the barrens, are largely bare of trees. This raised bog appears to be unique in northwestern Pennsylvania.

The trailhead for Pine Swamp is on the north side of PA 965, 3.9 miles east of I-79 and 1.0 mile west of PA 173 at Perrine Corners. Park along the highway as best you can.

The hike starts on an old logging road across the highway from a white house. The logging road is obvious but unblazed. Soon you pass a sawmill site, cross a pipe line swath, and then you come to the "Pine Swamp Natural Area" sign. Trees along this section are

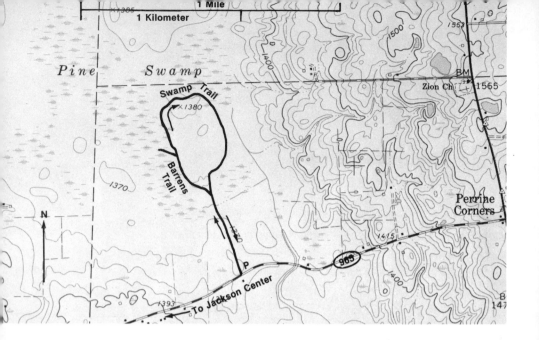

basswood, red maple and tulip.

Be quiet as you approach Wolf Creek, and you may flush a marsh hawk. Keep right along the top of an old beaver dam and step across the flowing water of Wolf Creek. Look for bladderwort, blue iris and marsh marigold here. At 0.4 mile (0.6 km) you reach the signed junction of the Swamp and Barrens trails. Turn left on the white-blazed Barrens Trail, which takes you past some white pines to another signed trail junction at 0.7 mile (1.1 km); this is where the Swamp Trail rejoins the Barrens Trail. Here the Barrens Trail proceeds ahead, but it is white-blazed, not yellow as indicated in the Conservancy brochure. Look out for poison ivy along this trail.

The wading soon begins but rarely over your knees, and at 0.8 mile (1.3 km) you reach the open central area of the barrens, where the high bush blueberries grow. The blazes end here, and if you are going to wander off berry picking or botanizing, take a good hard look at this entrance trail, so that you can find it again.

After filling your pack with blueberries, you could just retrace your steps. But to continue the hike, turn left on the Swamp Trail at the last trail junction. At 0.9 mile (1.5 km) the Swamp Trail leads you on to dry ground with hemlocks. You bear right at 1.1 miles (1.8 km), along the edge of a marsh, and soon leave the hemlocks and wade in. The going is very slow, and you must keep careful watch for the next blaze. The trail twists and turns, sometimes jumping from log to hummock to root. Trees growing here are largely gray birch. Part way across you encounter some rhododendron. At 1.3 miles (2.1 km) you reach reasonably dry land and turn right. Here the trail twists and turns in order to stay on dry land. At 1.7 miles (2.7 km) you turn left at the end of the logging road. This is the end of the blazing, and soon you are back at the first signed trail junction. Continue ahead and retrace your steps to your car, where you will want to rinse off the mud and change into those dry clothes.

Goddard-McKeever Trail

Distance: 3.2 miles (5.2 km)
Time: 2½ hours
Rise: 540 feet (165 m)
Highlights: Lake Wilhelm, McKeever
    Environmental Education Center
Maps: USGS 7½' Sandy Lake; state park map,
    McKeever Trail Guide (available at
    Environmental Education Center)

Maurice K. Goddard State Park, around Lake Wilhelm in Mercer County, honors a Penn State forestry professor who became head of the Pennsylvania Department of Forests and Waters in 1955. Dr. Goddard served in the cabinets of more governors than any one else in the history of the state. When the Department of Environmental Resources was created in 1971, he became secretary and served until 1979. One ambition of Dr. Goddard's was to have a state park within 40 kilometers of every citizen of the Commonwealth. Lake Wilhelm is a flood control reservoir named for Lawrence J. Wilhelm, director of the Mercer County Soil and Water Conservation District and a Mercer County commissioner.

Near Goddard Park is the McKeever Environmental Education Center named for Ivan McKeever, state conservationist from 1946 to 1968. The Center offers environmental education for students, preschool through college as well as adult workshops. Organized groups of six or more hikers should register with the Center at least one week in advance. It is unusual for state installations, even ones as close as Goddard and McKeever, to be linked by trail on public land.

The trailhead for this hike is a parking lot, just below the Lake Wilhelm dam. From the traffic light in Sandy Lake at the junction of US 62, PA 385, and PA 173, drive north on PA 173 for 0.5 mile and turn left on a gravel road. A small sign at this junction indicates the way to the dam. It is 0.7 mile further to the parking lot, which is on the right side of the road. Restrooms are provided here. Ordinary walking shoes are fine for this short hike on good paths.

To start the hike, bear left up the incline along the edge of the dam. At the top you get a view across the lower end of Lake Wilhelm. Cross the road, follow the trail into the woods, and then bear right. At 0.2 mile (0.3 km) you reach the overlook of Lake Wilhelm. A covered bench has been provided for you to sit and enjoy the view. To continue, turn sharp left and follow the trail along the edge of a field. Beware of poison ivy. Soon you bear left into the woods, and at 0.5 mile (0.8 km) you bear right on the trail to McKeever. The paved Patton Road is crossed at 0.6 mile (1.0 km), and just beyond you cross what appears to be an old railroad bed, as indicated by the cinders and narrow width. The trail next passes through a swamp, and several types of bog bridges have been employed to keep you from sinking into the mud.

At 0.8 mile (1.3 km) the trail crosses a lane, and a pair of stiles are used to climb over the fences bordering the lane. It appears that the stiles have replaced gates, which if left open, would allow livestock to escape. On the far side of the lane you cross an open meadow, and at the far side of the meadow, you enter the McKeever center. After passing under a pole line, you bear left at a trail junction toward Rocky Basin, a former recreation area.

Next you turn left on the Woodland Tapestry Trail at 1.4 miles (2.2 km). The Woodland Tapestry Trail is marked with a stylized star on the signs. Soon you reach Rocky Basin, where you could extend the hike by turning left on the Historical Trail, marked with a pick and shovel. The Historical Trail would take you past an old coal mine and the foundations of a farm homestead. If you continue on the Woodland Tapestry Trail, pause on the bridge over McCutcheon Run. The hemlock ravine, which starts just below the bridge, is well

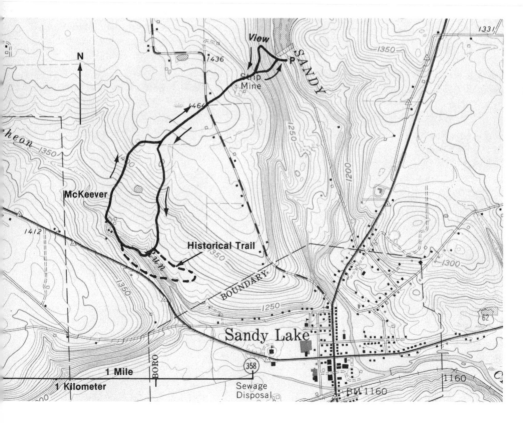

Corduroy Trail

worth inspection. Note that the current bridge is built on much older abutments. The Woodland Tapestry Trail then heads upstream along McCutcheon Run. Just after the historical trail comes in from the left at 1.7 miles (2.7 km), turn right at an unmarked junction, avoiding the old trail, which continues ahead.

Passing a junction with the Leisure Link Trail, you soon emerge between the auditorium and discovery buildings. Turn right and then left on the sidewalks to reach the small trailhead shelter at 1.9 miles (3.1 km). Here you pick up the Woodland Tapestry Trail again and follow it downhill to a crossing of McCutcheon Run. Beyond the bridge, turn left and then left again at 2.1 miles (3.4 km) to Goddard State Park. This trail traverses a stand of beech trees and then passes an outdoor auditorium before reaching another junction at 2.4 miles (3.9 km). Turn left here and retrace your steps to the trail junction just beyond Patton Road. If you don't mind a steep descent, turn right and cross an old road. Then pass by an old strip mine. The trail drops steeply to the junction near the park road. The parking lot and your car are just beyond.

Presque Isle State Park

Distance: 3.9 miles (6.3 km)
Time: 2 hours
Rise: 10 feet (3 m)
Highlights: Lake Erie, lighthouse
Maps: USGS 7½' Erie North; state park map

Presque Isle is a sand spit in the shallow waters of Lake Erie. To our eyes, it is part of the permanent landscape. But if we could take time-lapse photographs over a few hundred years, we would see it is actually moving. Beaches on the western side are washed away, only to become new land on the eastern side. Under the action of wind and waves, the entire pile of sand has moved east about 800 meters in the past century. Coming from the mainland, you pass through several centuries of plant succession. First are oak, sugar maple and hemlock—the climax vegetation. Then there are white pine, poplar, red maple and cedar—sunloving trees that provide shade for the shade-tolerant species that form the climax forest. Next, you leave the trees behind and reach an area covered with shrubs and other small plants. Finally, at the eastern tip, you come to an area where dunes and beaches have just been formed. This new land is stabilized by young poplars, whose roots anchor the moving sand.

Presque Isle has its share of human history as well. Commodore Perry's fleet was built here during the War of 1812. After defeating the British, Perry's flotilla remained at Misery Bay for the rest of the war. A full-sized replica of Perry's flagship, the "Niagara", is on display in downtown Erie.

To reach the park and trailhead from I-79, turn west on US 20 (26th Street), and then turn north on PA 832 (Peninsula Drive), which takes you out onto Presque Isle. At 1.5 miles beyond the park office, turn left and then right on Mill Road. Another 0.6 mile brings you to the trailhead for the Sidewalk Trail. Park along the road and head down the Sidewalk Trail. Ordinary walking shoes or sneakers are fine for this hike, but you will need some strong insect repellent. There is some poison ivy along the trail, but it is easily avoided.

First you pass the end of the unsigned Dead Pond Trail, which comes in from the left, and then you pass the Marsh Trail that diverges to the right. Trees growing along this section are red oak, red maple, chokecherry, pin oak, ash and willow. The Sidewalk Trail was once a nature trail, and some of the numbered posts still survive. However, the trail guide is no longer available.

Lake Erie

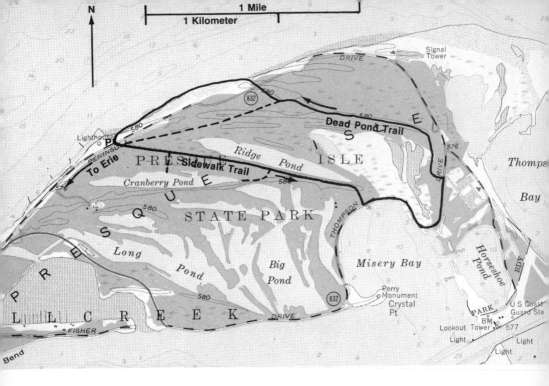

At 0.6 mile (1.0 km) the Fox Trail goes right, and soon you can see the open water of Ridge Pond to your left. The pond is a good habitat for ducks, and you may be able to hear them, even if you can't see them. Service berry grows along this section, and the fruit of the chokecherry is also edible. Chokecherries are extremely tart and really pucker up your mouth.

Soon the Sidewalk Trail turns right and ends at Thompson Road on the edge of Misery Bay where Perry's fleet was stationed. The Perry Monument can be seen across the bay. Turn left along Thompson Drive. Keep left, facing traffic, as you round the end of Niagara Pond. Here you find poplars growing along the bay. On the far side of the pond you pass gray birch and pitch pine.

At 1.9 miles (3.1 km) turn left onto the unsigned Bush Trail, opposite a road on the right. Deer tracks show that peo-

ple are not the only ones using the trails. Soon you turn left on the unsigned Dead Pond Trail. Like the Sidewalk Trail, this trail is mostly in the open, but whenever you pass through a patch of woods, the deerflies close in. Most insect repellents don't seem to bother deerflies.

At 2.9 miles (4.6 km) bear right at a fork in the trail. This is the B Trail, and it soon brings you out to the Pine Tree Road. Cross the road, proceed to the beach and bear left. Lake Erie is truly an inland sea. You can't see the other side. Erie and the other great lakes are the world's largest deposit of fresh water, outside Greenland.

Continue along the beach until you approach the lighthouse. The lighthouse isn't very high and just barely gets above the tree tops. This is your landmark to turn inland, and you should come out on the road within sight of your car.

Erie Extension Canal Towpath

Distance: 6.0 miles (9.6 km)
Time: 3 hours
Rise: 10 feet (3 m)
Highlights: Pymatuning Swamp; waterfowl
Maps: USGS 7½' Conneaut Lake, Hartstown;
    Sportsmen's Recreation map—State Game
    Lands No. 214

In the 1830's and '40's, Pennsylvania underwent a vast program of canal building. By the 1840's, canals stretched from the Delaware River to Lake Erie. These canals were not all built to the same standards. Locks on different canals were of different lengths and widths. Two rail links, the Columbia to Philadelphia Railroad in the east and the Allegheny Portage Railroad in the west, were also included. A great deal of loading and unloading was required, making the canal system uncompetitive with the fast-developing railroads. By the 1850's, the railroads had gained the upper hand. While some canals continued in use until the twentieth century, most were abandoned in the nineteenth. Most of the abandoned canals were bought by the very railroads they had competed with. Some were destroyed in the construction of railroads and highways, others by a century of floods and the growth of trees and other vegetation. Very few old canals, then, are found on public lands.

One part of the Erie Extension Canal and its towpath came into public ownership by accident, with the development of adjacent Pymatuning State Park. The Erie Extension Canal originally ran from the Ohio River up Beaver Valley to Erie, with a side canal down French Creek to the Allegheny River at Franklin. It was completed in 1844. The canal crossed the backwaters of Pymatuning Swamp. As the land was flat, no locks were required.

The canal towpath across the eastern arm of Pymatuning cut off a 600 acre lake, which served as a reservoir for the canal. Canals used water every time a boat went through a lock. The old canals probably lost a good deal of water through leakage as well. If a canal ran out of water, the first boat to run aground blocked the channel and halted traffic in both directions.

The old towpath makes a very different sort of hike. There is no problem in following it. And while most trails require people to walk single file, this one is wide enough for two people to walk side by side. It's a good trail for a long talk with a friend.

There are a great many birds along the trail. Chickadees chatter from the trees, herons stalk the shallows,

kingfishers dart into the water, and a great honking over the swamp heralds the approach of a flight of geese. Don't forget your binoculars.

Although I expected the insects to be a real problem, the hike is mostly out in the open, and I didn't have to use repellent, even on a warm day in July. Almost any sort of shoes should be adequate for the excellent footway on this hike.

The trailhead is reached from US 322, 5.0 miles west of the junction with PA 18 in Conneaut lake and just east of Hartstown. Turn north at the east side of the overpass which crosses the Bessemer and Lake Erie Railroad. This gravel road is very rough at first, so take it slow and thread your way around the mud puddles at the bottom of the slope. Turn right at the bottom and continue. The cinder road swings away from the railroad, and at 1.0 mile from US 322 you reach a gate and game commission parking lot.

To start the hike, dodge around the gate and head out along the old towpath. Note the difference in water levels on the two sides of the towpath. The water on the right is almost two meters higher than the water on the left.

Trees along your route are chokecherry, aspen, red maple, elm, cucumber, cottonwood, walnut, locust, red oak, white oak, hickory, sassafrass, willow and apple. Sumac also grows here as does wild strawberry and poison ivy. The game commission mows the route, however, so the poison ivy does not reach the path.

At 0.5 mile (0.8 km) you cross a bridge over the dam that controls the level of the old reservoir. Here you see the difference in water levels clearly. This is a favorite spot of fishermen. In the reservoir water lilies abound, but on the other side the ground alternates be-

Open Water in the Old Canal Reservoir

tween marsh and woods. Look for deer tracks on the path. When I turned around once, I found a doe following me.

At 1.5 miles (2.4 km) you reach the site of an old bridge across the canal. A couple of planks across the trickle provide access for fishermen. At 1.8 miles (2.9 km) you see farms along the far side of the valley, and at 3.0 miles (4.8 km) you reach the vehicle gate next to PA 285. Along the way you have crossed an unmarked corner of Pymatuning State Park. Ahead, the old towpath continues across private land before returning to the route of the Bessemer and Lake Erie Railroad. Turn and retrace your steps along the towpath to your car.

Two Mile Run County Park

Distance: 6.2 miles (10.0 km)
Time: 3½ hours
Rise: 660 feet (200 m)
Highlight: A walk around the lake
Maps: USGS 7½' Franklin; county park map

Most county parks have picnic tables and baseball diamonds. Two Mile Run Park in Venango County offers much more. It has swimming and boating on Justus Lake, family and group camping areas, horseback riding, ski touring and hiking. The park was started in 1969 with funding from a variety of sources. The lake was completed by 1974. The hiking trails were built by Boy Scout troops, nature study groups and the neighborhood Youth Corps.

Two Mile Run Park is most easily reached from PA 417. The turnoff is 6.2 miles north of Franklin and 2.2 miles south of Dempseytown. Turn east for 1.6 miles, passing the park office, and then turn south for 0.9 mile to the beach area. Park in the upper lot near the activities center. Ordinary walking shoes are adequate, but hiking boots wouldn't be out of place.

Cross the road on the far side of the activities center and start off on the cross-country ski trail, which is marked by blue discs with red arrows. Soon the Crosby Trail comes in from the right, and the footway becomes much clearer. The presence of may apples along this

section of the trail hints of other spring wild flowers, as well. At 0.3 mile (0.5 km) you cross the Bea-Cam Trail, on which you will return at the end of your hike. Shortly beyond this junction, you cross a road and pole line. The ski trail turns to the right, but you continue into the woods and then keep right where George's Trail diverges to the left. You climb up the side of a hill, passing a white pine along the way. After descending the far side, you continue ahead on a swath at 1.1 miles (1.7 km). This swath is marked as the cross-country ski trail, but the slope to the right looks suitable for experts only. The Black Gum Trail goes left at this junction to the Top O'Flats picnic area.

Soon another swath comes in from the right. Continuing ahead, you pass jack pine and a scarlet oak "wolf tree." A wolf tree is a large tree that instead of growing straight and tall, spreads wide and shades out all competition. Norway spruce and aspen are found along the trail before you pass a vehicle gate and turn left on a dirt road at 1.5 miles (2.4 km). The dirt road takes you across a stream and then up to a gravel

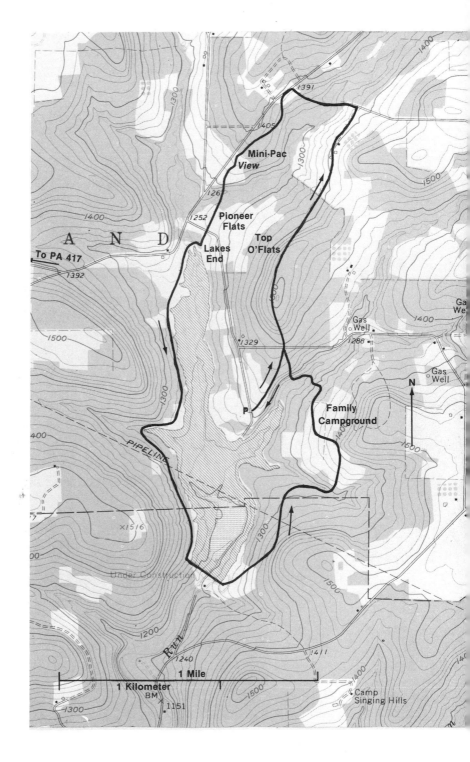

Mini-Pac
View

Pioneer
Flats

Lakes
End

Top
O'Flats

To PA 417

Family
Campground

Gas
Well

Gas
Well

Ga
We

PIPELINE

N

Under Construction

Run

BM

Camp
Singing Hills

1 Mile

1 Kilometer

road where you turn left on the Roadside Trail, which goes along the edge of a spruce plantation next to the road.

Soon the trail bears left, away from the gravel road and follows a series of old roads before emerging at the Mini-Pac picnic area at 2.2 miles (3.5 km). There is a view across the park from this point, but the trail is difficult to find where it leaves this open area. All you can do is head for the obvious hole in the trees at the far side. The trail drops down a steep bank and then crosses a footbridge over a stream to reach the Pioneer Flats picnic area. Make your way across the open field and cross the paved road. Proceed to the Lakes End picnic area and go all the way to the lake's edge before turning right to the footbridge over the inlet. Look for herons and other water birds along here.

Continue around the marina, and at the far side bear left on the Lake's End Trail, crossing another footbridge. Beyond the stream, you pass through a meadow growing up into white pine, and then reenter the woods. At 3.4 miles (5.5 km) a ski trail goes off to the right, but you continue ahead. The swimming beach is across the lake from here. Soon you cross a side trail and a stream, beyond which you may spot some trees felled by beavers. At 3.8 miles (6.1 km) you jog left across a pipe line swath. Soon you bear left on an old road marked with ski trail markers, and shortly you turn left across the top of the dam. You can see the entire lake as you cross. Toward the far side of the dam, turn left, cross the dry spillway and enter the woods on the cross-country ski trail.

At 4.7 miles (7.5 km) you bear left off the old road, and soon you keep right at a fork in the trail. Next you cross a stream on a log bridge, and then climb, emerging at a corner of the family campground at 5.4 miles (8.6 km). Turn left and follow the road through the campground. On the far side of the campground, turn left on the Bea-Cam Trail. Cross the footbridge and use the switchbacks to climb the steep slope beyond. Turn left at 5.9 miles (9.5 km) on the combined Crosby and cross-country ski trails and retrace your steps to the parking lot at the activities center.

A map of the park showing at least eight more hiking trails can be obtained from the park office (which you pass on the way to the trailhead).

Allegheny Gorge

Distance: 6.3 miles (10.1 km)
Time: 3½ hours
Rise: 560 feet (170 m)
Highlights: Old iron furnace, view of
   Allegheny River
Maps: USGS 7½' Kennerdell; state forest trail
   maps for Allegheny Tract

In the 1970's the state purchased over 3,000 acres along the Allegheny River in Venango County for a new state park to be called Allegheny Gorge. The tract included some ten kilometers along the Allegheny River where it has cut a canyon, more than 150 meters deep, through the plateau. The land had been heavily used in the past, first for subsistence farming, then for charcoal iron manufacturing and, more recently, for gas and oil drilling. Funds to develop the new park did not materialize, and the land became part of Clear Creek State Forest. With an adjoining tract of State Game Lands 39, the area is about 4,000 acres. Cooperation between the Bureau of Forestry, the State Game Commission and the Grove City College Outing Club is producing a network of hiking trails and cross-country ski trails above and along the Allegheny River. One impressive overlook has been cleared, and another is planned.

Allegheny Gorge is most easily reached from new PA 8. Exit on PA 308 and turn northwest toward Pearl. Turn right on old PA 8 for 0.4 mile and then turn right on Dennison Run Road (T-371). Continue east for 1.7 miles and then turn right for 1.1 miles to a game commission parking lot at the end of the road. Hiking boots or good walking shoes should be fine for this hike.

To start, head south from the parking lot along the gated game commission management road. The game commission has permitted trail signs to be posted but hasn't permitted the trail blazing to be extended across its lands. At 0.3 mile (0.4 km) you bear left on an old road that leads into the woods. Old earthworks are encountered at 0.8 mile (1.2 km). They are thought to be bog iron pits, which provided iron ore for the several local furnaces. The pits can be followed for long distances at this elevation as they followed the outcrop of ore. You cross the boundary of state forest land at 0.9 mile (1.4 km). From here on, the trail is marked with orange paint blazes. Soon you turn right for Bullion Run Iron Furnace. You will return on the other blazed trail at this junction. Continue past a spring to the right of

View of Allegheny River

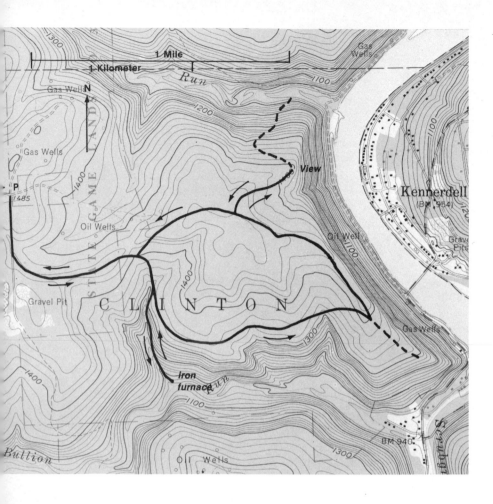

the trail, and then cross a bridge over a small stream in a hemlock grove. Bear right at 1.2 miles (1.9 km) for the iron furnace. The trail follows an old road down a nameless tributary of Bullion Run. Unlike other parts of the state, here charcoal was made at the furnace rather than out in the woods. This road was used to bring the necessary iron ore and wood. Apparently the lure of hauling wood to the furnace was too much for the farmers. Subsistence farming collapsed in favor of a cash economy. When you reach the bottom, bear left along or above Bullion Run,

and you soon come to the ruins of the stack. The stonework is in fairly bad shape, so don't attempt to climb. On the far side, so much of the wall has collapsed that you can see the core of the furnace. From here, pig iron was hauled to the Allegheny for shipment to Pittsburgh aboard the white pine rafts that floated down from Tionesta.

After you've seen the furnace, climb back up the trail through the hemlock grove, ignoring a yellow-blazed trail, and turn right at the top of the hill. This trail takes you through open woods at the edge of the plateau above Bullion Run, and presently you see the ruins of old oil wells. The metal rods crossing the trail indicate that a central engine was used to pump a number of wells simultaneously. It's said a steam engine was used to pump these wells, which would make the installation older than the one on display at the Drake Well Museum near Titusville.

At 3.1 miles (5.0 km) turn left on the old Kennerdell Road, which goes along the edge of the plateau above the Allegheny. A number of old trail markings can be seen along this section, including outsize carpet tacks. The Grove City College Outing Club has marked trails here since the 1930's. Turn right at 4.1 miles (6.5 km) to reach the Dennison Point overlook and then right again at 4.5 miles (7.2 km). Ahead, this trail descends 400 feet into Dennison Run Valley, an optional side trip.

The overlook is a good 400 feet above the Allegheny. Part of the village of Kennerdell can be seen across the river, and you can also see far upriver.

Retracing your steps to the old Kennerdell Road, turn right and continue past extensive stands of mountain laurel. The oak with the deeply furrowed bark is chestnut oak and indicates the dryness of this site. At 5.2 miles (8.3 km) turn left, and you soon reach the junction with the trail you came in on near the state forest boundary. Bear right, avoiding an unmarked trail, and retrace your steps to your car in the game commission parking lot.

Other trails are available in the Allegheny tract of Clear Creek State Forest. One follows the river from the bridgehead across from Kennerdell upstream to Fisherman Cove near Clark Run. Another follows the ridge north of Dennison Run out to parking areas near the road junction known as Five Points. A new overlook of the Allegheny will be cut along this second trail, above the bend south of Whitherup Island.

50

Oil Creek State Park

Distance: 12.6 miles (20.2 km)
Time: 7½ hours
Rise: 1,510 feet (460 m)
Highlights: World's first oil pipe line;
  Oil Creek Gorge
Maps: USGS 7½' Titusville South, Oil City

This hike takes you along historic and beautiful Oil Creek south of Titusville. Oil seeps have occurred in this valley since prehistoric times. Indians dug pits to collect the oil. Here in 1859, "Colonel" Edwin Drake drilled the world's first oil well. By good fortune, Drake struck oil only 23 meters down. Most of the producing oil sand was 150 meters below the valley floor. But Drake's luck deserted him, and he died poor, while others made fortunes along Oil Creek and at the ghost town of Pithole, just to the east. Some wells still produce oil nearby, and one has produced continuously since 1861. Pennsylvania rocks hold onto their oil so tenaciously that some of the last producing wells or dry land may turn out to be not too far from here.

The oil boom of the 1860's produced much of the technology still in use today. From the North Slope of Alaska to the floor of the North Sea to the far reaches of Siberia, inventions made here in Pennsylvania are still in use.

Much of this historic region is now contained in Oil Creek State Park, which stretches from PA 8 north to the Drake

Well historic site. Ironically, perhaps, two attractions of this park, which commemorates the dawn of the Petroleum Age, are a bicycle trail, between the Drake Well and the park headquarters, and the Oil Creek Hiking Trail.

Eventually, the Oil Creek Trail will make a loop of about 30 miles, crossing Oil Creek at the ghost town of Petroleum Center and on a yet-to-be-built footbridge south of the Drake Well. The Western Pennsylvania Conservancy is to pay for this footbridge. But the trail has in large part been the retirement project of Ray Gerrard of Titusville. On the western side of the park, trail access will be provided to Oil Creek Camp Resort, a private campground. A primitive campsite may be opened to hikers on the eastern side of the park. These will permit a three-day backpack on the Oil Creek Trail. Until then, the Oil Creek Trail is limited to day hiking. This hike follows the eastern side of the loop from near the Drake Well almost to the park headquarters. It requires a car

Log Bridge

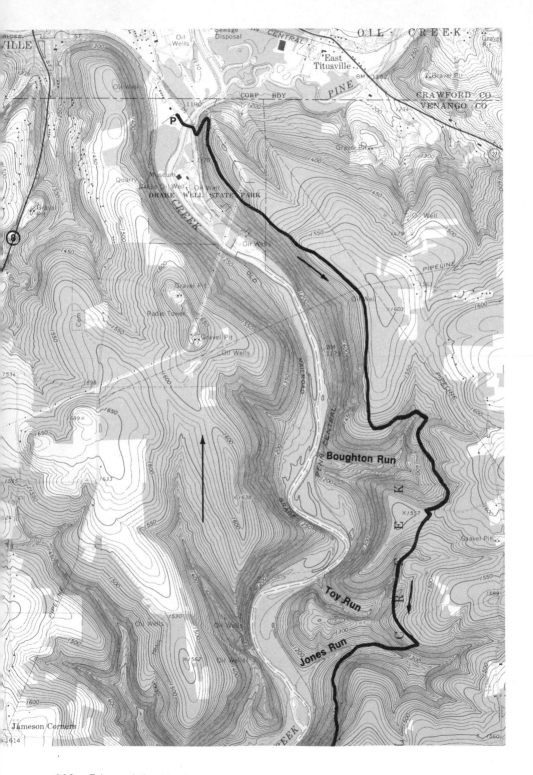

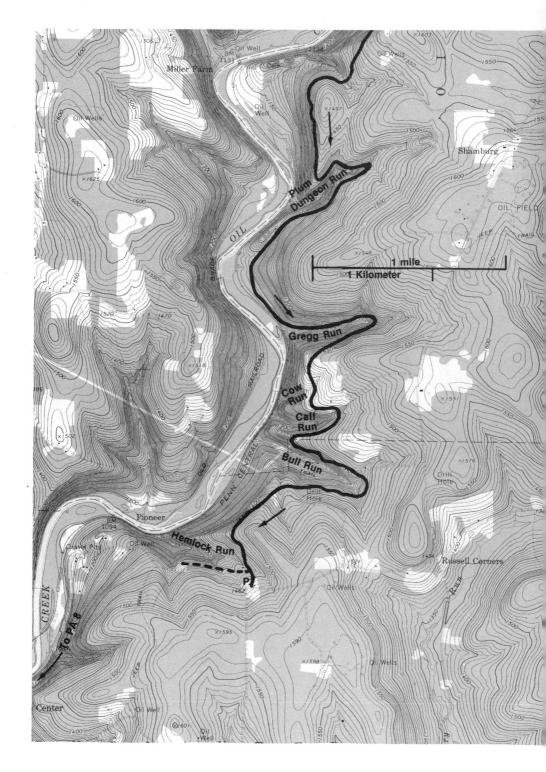

Miller Farm
Shamburg
OIL FIELD
Plum
Dungeon Run
OIL
GRADE
1 mile
1 Kilometer
RAILROAD
Gregg Run
Cow
Run
Calf
Run
Bull Run
OLD
PENN CENTRAL
Drill
Hole
Pioneer
Drill
Hole
Gravel Pit
Oil Well
Hemlock Run
Russell Corners
CREEK
To PA 8
Center

shuttle. Due to length and many wet spots, hiking boots are required.

From PA 8, about 5 miles south of Titusville, turn east at the sign for Oil Creek State Park (LR 600455). Follow this road 3.6 miles down into Oil Creek Valley and through the site of Petroleum Center, in its heyday perhaps the wildest town in the state. The steps of the bank are the only obvious sign of a town that once entertained President Grant. Cross the bridge over Oil Creek and then turn left on Petroleum Center Road (Town Road 599) and follow it for 2.0 miles to a parking area on the north side of the road, just past the junction with T-586. Leave one car here and continue east for 1.0 mile to Russell Corners. Turn left here on White City Road (T-600) for 5.7 miles and then turn left again on Drake Well Road (T-602). Follow Drake Well Road down into Oil Creek Valley, crossing Oil Creek again, and park in the bicycle trail area just beyond the bridge.

To start your hike on the yellow-blazed Oil Creek Trail, walk back across Oil Creek and turn right on the abandoned Conrail grade. Just 100 feet down this grade, turn sharp left and cross the deep ditch on a fallen tree with a steel cable to help your balance. Immediately the trail turns left on an old road to Pithole. At the next right turn there is a view of Titusville from the power line swath, just off the trail. At 0.8 mile (1.3 km) you cross the power line swath, which provides a view across Oil Creek Valley. A planned loop trail would diverge here and return to the Drake Well historic site near the trailhead. Beyond the swath, you cross an area that burned in May 1982 when a trash fire got away. Cross an old oil well site and ascend slowly to the high point on the east side of Oil Creek.

Next, you jog right across a natural gas pipe line to reach a trail junction at 1.8 miles (2.8 km). When the footbridge across Oil Creek has been completed, it will be reached by a trail going straight ahead at this junction. But you turn left, uphill, to continue along the east side. There's an intermittent spring left of the trail at 2.3 miles (3.7 km), and at 2.7 miles (4.3 km) you enter a hemlock grove. Next you turn right and cross the northeast branch of Boughton Run. Soon you cross another branch, turn right and cross the southeast branch on a log bridge. You then continue on a logging road which leads above Boughton Falls. Oil Creek Gorge is of postglacial origin, hence the steep valleys and waterfalls characteristic of a young drainage system.

At 3.5 miles (5.6 km) you cross another stream, and immediately beyond, there is a spring to the left of the trail. Next you turn left at a switch-back and shortly turn right at the top of a hill. Soon you pass through a red pine plantation and then turn downstream along Toy Run, crossing it at 4.1 miles (6.5 km).

At 4.5 miles (7.2 km) you turn right on an old road, and at 5.0 miles (8.0 km) you turn left onto trail. Soon you cross a small stream first and then Jones Run itself. Beyond Jones Run you climb to the top of the hill where you pass a sawmill site. Then bear right off the old road, passing a pipe spring to the left and reaching Miller Farm Road at 6.1 miles (9.7 km). This road offers the only possibility for shortening this hike. However, parking is limited.

Beyond the road, the trail climbs to the Van Syckle pipe line at 6.3 miles (10.0 km). This was the world's first successful pipe line. Only five centimeters in diameter, eight kilometers long and leaking at every joint, it carried oil from Pithole to storage tanks at the Miller farm on the railroad. Realizing its threat, the teamsters attacked the pipe line at night and tore it apart. The owners hired gunmen who were stationed at 400 meter intervals with orders to shoot anything that moved. When the teamsters found the pipe line too well defended, they set fire to the storage tanks at Miller farm. Today, pipe lines stretch across Alaska and from Siberia to Western Europe. But this was the first. Now only a shallow trench remains.

Continuing on the trail, you turn left at 6.6 miles (10.6 km) to circle the head of Plum Dungeon Run. A side trail will be built to the falls. At 6.9 miles (11.0 km) you turn right on an old road and soon pass a spring to the right of the trail. Next you cross a couple of small streams. You descend slowly, and at 8.2 miles (13.1 km) you can see the abandoned Conrail grade to your right. The trail continues along the bottoms on old roads before turning left and starting the long climb along Gregg Run. Gregg Run had its oil wells, too, and ruins of pump jacks and stock tanks can be seen from the trail. At 9.2 miles (14.7 km) you cross Gregg Run and then continue past a beautiful stand of hemlocks growing on the steep slope below the trail. The removal of a few trees at the top of the hill would open views up and down Oil Creek Gorge.

Next you turn right, passing some old pump houses. At 10.1 miles (16.2 km) turn right again and cross Calf Run. Then turn right once more onto an old road that leads you under a small power line to a view across Bull Run Valley. At 10.6 miles (16.9 km) turn sharply left and head east above Bull Run, crossing under the power line again. Later you cross a couple of tributaries of Bull Run, and then you bear left off the old road. At 11.5 miles (18.4 km) you reach an old and very deep oil well next to the trail. A small stone dropped into it can be heard to hit the sides repeatedly before making a splash deep beneath the earth. Next you cross an old road and turn first left, and then right. At 12.1 miles (19.4 km) turn right and then left. Soon you turn right again, and at 12.5 miles (20.0 km) where the yellow blazes bear right, you continue ahead on the unblazed old road to the trailhead parking along T-599.

While you are at Oil Creek, visit the Drake Well Museum and historic site. The museum contains many exhibits from the early days of the Petroleum Age, including a reconstruction of Drake's Well.

Guidebooks from Backcountry Publications

Written for people of all ages and experience, these popular and carefully prepared books feature detailed trail directions, notes on historical and natural points of interest, maps and photographs.

For Pennsylvania—

Fifty Hikes in Eastern Pennsylvania. By Carolyn Hoffman $8.95

Fifty Hikes in Central Pennsylvania. By Tom Thwaites $7.95

For Central New York—

25 Walks in the Finger Lakes Region. By William P. Ehling $5.95

25 Ski Tours in Central New York. By William P. Ehling $5.95

Canoeing Central New York. By William P. Ehling $8.95

20 Bicycle Tours in the Finger Lakes. By Mark Roth and Sally Walters $6.95

In the *Fifty Hikes* series—

Fifty Hikes in the Adirondacks. By Barbara McMartin $8.95

Fifty Hikes in Connecticut. By Gerry and Sue Hardy $7.95

Fifty Hikes in Maine (rev. ed.). By John Gibson $8.95

Fifty Hikes in Massachusetts. By John Brady and Brian White $8.95

Fifty Hikes in Vermont. By Ruth and Paul Sadlier $7.95

Fifty Hikes in the White Mountains (NH) (3rd rev. ed.). By Daniel Doan $8.95

Fifty More Hikes in Maine. By Cloe Catlett $8.95

Fifty More Hikes in New Hampshire (rev. ed.). By Daniel Doan $8.95

Other outdoor recreation books—

Dan Doan's Fitness Program for Hikers and Cross-Country Skiers. By Daniel Doan $4.95

A Year with New England's Birds: A Guide to Twenty-Five Field Trips. By Sandy Mallett $5.95

Available from bookstores, sporting goods stores, or the Publisher. For complete descriptions of these and other books in our *20 Bicycle Tours, 25 Walks, 25 Ski Tours, Canoeing* and *Fishing* series, write to: Backcountry Publications, Inc., P.O. Box 175, Woodstock, Vermont 05091